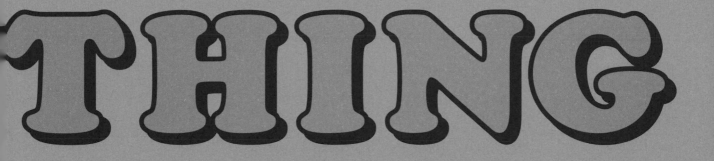

THING

A WISE SONS COOKBOOK
for Jews Who Like Food *and* Food Lovers Who Like Jews

BY EVAN BLOOM
& RACHEL LEVIN

Illustrations by George McCalman
Photographs by Maren Caruso

CHRONICLE BOOKS
SAN FRANCISCO

Text copyright © 2020 by Beck and Bloom, LLC.
Photographs copyright © 2020 by Maren Caruso.
Illustrations by George McCalman.

Library of Congress Cataloging-in-Publication Data available.
ISBN 978-1-4521-7874-5
Prop styling by Jillian Knox.
Food styling by Robyn Valarik and Kristene Loayza.
Design by McCalmanCo: George McCalman and Aliena Cameron.
The photographer wishes to thank Jennifer Thomas, Josh Lewis,
Carolyn Schneider, and Daniel Hurlburt.
Manufactured in China.

10 9 8 7 6 5 4 3 2 1

Chronicle books and gifts are available at special quantity
discounts to corporations, professional associations, literacy
programs, and other organizations. For details and discount
information, please contact our premiums department at
corporatesales@chroniclebooks.com or at 1-800-759-0190.

Chronicle Books LLC
680 Second Street
San Francisco, CA 94107
www.chroniclebooks.com

For our parents,
and their parents

A Jewish Life in Meals

a.k.a. the

TABLE OF CONTENTS

THE EARLY YEARS

THE AWKWARD YEARS

THE YOUNG-ADULTING YEARS

THE ALL-GROWN-UP YEARS

THE SNOWBIRD YEARS

Recipe List

INTRODUCTION
(the genesis of this book)

I'M AT WISE SONS DELI, in San Francisco's Mission District, slurping a bowl of matzo ball soup while the owners give me a convincing spiel about a book that doesn't exist yet—but should.

"It would be about Jews and food," Evan Bloom began, speaking on behalf of his partners: his brother, Ari, and his buddy Leo. "OK, not just another book about Jewish food, there are plenty of those—but about Jews and food. Get it? Do you have thoughts about Jews and food?" Do I, a Jewish food writer raised in a suburban home where platters of tongue and boxes of Entenmann's crumb cake poured like rain, have thoughts about Jews and food? Oh yes, I assured them, I had thoughts. Many thoughts.

"Good," Evan said. "That's what we wanted to hear, because we want to probe the depths of this subject. Go where no Jew has gone before. We don't want it to be a standard cookbook, per se," he explained. "Something more along the lines of the *Bar Mitzvah Disco* (2005)?" I suggested. "Yes!" Evan replied. But for bagels and brisket and babka and the people who eat them, we decided. With photos and illustrations and shared memories and schmaltz. And food, lots of food. "Will you write it with us? Bring home a dozen bagels and think about it. What kind of shmear do you want? ('You mean cream cheese?' I, a native East Coaster, replied.) Ari, get her the shmear with horseradish. ('I do love horseradish.') Where did you go to camp? ('Basically the same one as you, but in New Hampshire.') How was the food there? ('I liked the Dixie cups of Manischewitz on Shabbat—does that

count?') Did you know Adam Goldberg? ('Of course I knew Adam Goldberg.')"

I didn't need to think about it for long. Soon, I returned to Wise Sons' Twenty-Fourth Street deli—a twenty-first century, Califortified version of the New York staple—for inspiration. And brunch. And the first thing I noticed: There was not a guy in this place who didn't have a beard. (And there were a lot of guys in the place.)

There was also not a single diner with blonde hair, which is neither here nor there—other than to say that it appeared, at first, to be a deli filled with traditional deli-going types: i.e., Ashkenazi Jews. That is, until a dude sporting a turban strolled in and ordered lox, eggs, and onions. Then an Asian American man came calling for two dozen bagels, followed by an African American woman with dreads (as long as co-owner Leo Beckerman's used to be), craving a hunk of babka.

Of course, there was no shortage of stereotypes: a pair of tiny elderly ladies complaining about the wait; a New York expat mulling the Big Macher sandwich versus the corned beef; a mother-daughter duo digging into a plate of latkes with house-made applesauce, two months before Hanukkah.

After all, at Wise Sons, every day is a day to devour Jewish food. And, well, for those of us who are Jewish, every day is a day to devour.

···

AS JEWS WE CAN SAY THIS: Our people—in general—tend to lack certain life skills. We can't fix our own cars or repair our own appliances. We can't talk without yelling or walk without talking or hide our feelings or help but feel anxious. But, if there's one thing pretty much every Jew can do, it's eat.

And we do. With more fervor and focus than most. More than Italians? (Hard to believe, but yes. Although Bubbe's brisket probably wasn't as good as Nonna's meatballs.) More than Asians? (Yes. Even a Chinese wedding banquet isn't as excessive as a Florida gated-community clubhouse buffet.) More than most Episcopalians? (God, yes. A dried-out holiday ham flanked by five string beans does not a feast make.)

Two guys named Sean Altman and Rob Tannenbaum once wrote a song called "They Tried To Kill Us, We Survived, Let's Eat," performed by bands like Jewmongous and Good for the Jews. It was intended to usurp "Dayenu" as Passover's top hit. It didn't, but it does pretty much speak to every Jewish holiday, to Jews' centuries-old relationship with food.

No doubt, thousands of years of persecution and near starvation have seeped into our subconscious, contributing to our modern-day obsession with what to eat, when to eat, how to eat. There's got to be some deep-seated connection between our great-great-greats' painstaking commitment to keeping kosher and our picky, particular eating habits. (Ode

> ...at Wise Sons, every day is a day to devour Jewish food. And, well, for those of us who are Jewish, every day is a day to devour.

to Jew Nora Ephron, who penned Sally's famed diner-order diatribe in *When Harry Met Sally*.)

Then there are our it's-my-way-or-the-highway feelings about Jewish food in general. "You can't be a deli if you serve milk and meat!" customers at Wise Sons will declare. "You call these Manhattan half-sours!?" they complain. "Seriously, 'kale salad' at a Jewish deli? Oy. What's next, kosher kombucha?" they'll email. (See The Kvetching Department, page 218.) People walk into Wise Sons, into all delicatessens, with their own food memories, with preferences that have been ingrained since childhood. And those are not easy to shake. It's why Wise Sons' menu wisely includes this printed caveat with their matzo ball soup: "Not as good as your bubbe's."

Our lives, as Jews, revolve around food in a way that's at once fanatical, logical, and comical, and, to be honest, kind of pathological. Especially when family is in town. Meals are plotted with the care and calculation of a presidential campaign. While spreading the cream cheese on our bagels, we discuss where we should go for lunch; while the Russian dressing drips from our Reubens, we ruminate over dinner reservations; while arguing over the best way to get to the airport in the morning, we wonder if we'll have time to pick up egg-and-cheese sandwiches on the way. (We won't.)

Of course, this laser focus on food—on both being well fed and feeding others—is not unique to Jews. Indians and Iranians, Chinese and Koreans, we're all passionate about scoring prime reservations and packing plenty of snacks and serving abundant platters. God forbid someone goes hungry: Eating—along with studying and practicing and striving and surviving—it's an immigrant thing. Whether we came to America last year or last century, our roots run deep. Food is life, our need to overorder is real.

Chinese takeout, at least in my family, is ordered amid hot debate, a pen-in-hand process presided over by my father, while my mother (who "doesn't do Chinese") barks in the background, "How many are you planning to feed, Danny?" He then shrugs and proceeds to order fourteen dishes for our nuclear family of four, including sweet-and-sour pork. "Really, Danny? Pork?"

The fact that Sunday night Chinese is more of a ritual in most Jewish-American households than, say, reciting the HaMotzi before supper says a lot about who we are today, about what ties us together as a people.

Amy Schumer sums it up well in her book *The Girl with the Lower Back Tattoo* (2017), in her list of "Things You Don't Know About Me." Coming in at Number Twelve: "I don't go to temple anymore, but I like that I'm Jewish, and I enjoy the grossest Jewish food, like whitefish salad and gefilte fish."

And that's the thing: For so long, Jewish food was poo-pooed, especially by those who weren't Jewish. We loved it anyway, of course, because it was what we knew, because our mothers and grandmothers made it. Their creations were hardly gourmet, but they were hearty and holy, in a Heinz chili sauce kind of way.

American Jews growing up in the '70s, '80s, and '90s—like me and Evan and his fellow Wise Sons—remember when Maxwell House, Hydrox, and Del Monte canned-fruit Jell-O molds reigned.

Our grandmothers' briskets were dry and gray, their matzo balls as dense as bricks, their desserts rarely, if ever, home-made. "Unless you count Safta Rickey's Passover sponge cake, ripped from a recipe right off the back of the box," says Evan. Or the Manischewitz macaroons brought by a cranky aunt. (The chocolate ones were always, disappointingly, no better than the coconut.) Either way, Amy Schumer is right: There *was* nothing more gross in the entire world than gefilte fish.

···

THIS CASUAL, CONTEMPORARY, LIGHTHEARTED TAKE on a book about Jewish food is decidedly Wise Sons. Evan and Leo were the nice Jewish boys, after all, who, bemoan-ing the dearth of real-deal pastrami in the Bay Area, decided to make their own in their backyards, liked how it tasted, and, in 2011, said, "What the hell, let's try a pop-up!" They took over a nondescript spot on Valencia Street, and I was an early and instantly loyal customer. I even wrote the very first piece about this very first pop-up deli, for the *New York Times*, which apparently made their parents quite proud.

These are the next generation of deli guys who bucked centuries of family holiday tradition and hosted a sold-out Seder later that spring, inviting a bunch of strangers to a hip San Francisco cafe, where everyone was dressed in jeans and drinking wine—good wine—and listening to fresh-faced Leo recite the plagues while *The Ten Commandments*, the classic 1956 film starring Charlton Heston as Moses, played on a projector on the back wall.

It was the night I realized, Wait, Passover could be fun! Jewish holidays could be fun! Gefilte fish doesn't have to come congealed in a jar. Gefilte fish could taste good! Brisket could taste good! Wise Sons made me realize Jewish food, thousands of miles and three decades from my suburban Massachusetts childhood, might actually be something far better than merely edible. Moreover, Jewish food might actually be something enjoyed by people who—gasp—aren't even Jewish.

Jewish food might actually be something enjoyed by people who—gasp—aren't even Jewish.

...

We are basically under obligation, by birthright, to pile our plates high.

FROM THEIR EARLY DAYS COOKING for friends at UC Berkeley, Leo and Evan had a passion not just for corned beef but also community. Reinvigorating Jewish food with local-organic California ingredients, they gave new life to old staples, instantly drawing lines that rivaled the DMV's in both length and diversity for their pastrami and potato latkes and chocolate babka.

A decade or so later, Wise Sons has six storefronts strong in the Bay Area and one in Tokyo, products on grocery shelves from Bi-Rite to Whole Foods, and plans to expand. Wise Sons has its eye on the future, but its heart in history. Yet while nostalgia may fuel Wise Sons, it doesn't define it. And the same rings true for me, when I'm eating there. I feel the presence of my past, too. I'm just not stuck in it.

And neither is Wise Sons' food. Take their kugel (page 171): To conceive it, Evan collected recipes from family, from friends, from old Temple Beth Torah Sisterhood cookbooks, and then called in a Catholic cook who'd never had the classic eggy Ashkenazi noodle dish. "I wanted to look at it through an unbiased lens," he explained. They talked, and tasted, and tinkered. The secret? Yogurt and a healthy splash of OJ.

Wise Sons' philosophy is to preserve our past, and make it taste better. Not unlike the way Jews of our generation approach Judaism today: We respect our traditions, but make them our own. Which includes writing this book about Jewish food that—feh!—might include a recipe for a cheeseburger, and maybe even make you laugh.

"I want it to be fun to read and fun to write," Evan insisted, over "Semite" sandwiches (crispy pastrami, runny egg, melted Swiss, and mustard on rye), weeks after he proposed collaborating.

It was our first official brainstorm meeting. I agreed. "It should be easy enough," I said. "When Jews and food get together, it is fun." (And often funny.) "I want your friend George McCalman to illustrate and design it," Evan said. "Me, too!" I replied. I'd brought George—Caribbean born, Brooklyn raised, gay, black, gentile—to his very first Seder, which was also that first Wise Sons Seder. George had had the best time. "I'm finally with my people!" he'd exclaimed over the fourth glass of wine.

So, if this wasn't going to be a traditional book about Jewish food, what was it going to be, exactly? We discussed with our agent, Danielle Svetcov, an M.O.T. herself. And collectively, over bagels, of course, we decided.

Two years later, after much talking, noshing, laughing, and crying, we present to you *Eat Something*, for Jews who like food and food lovers who like Jews. Consider it a scrapbook, of sorts, covering life's main events, filled with anecdotes and essays, illustrations and archival images, and all the recipes every good Jew or bad Jew or wannabe Jew needs.

Lest you think we are total gluttons, it turns out that, say, roaming from french fry station to meatball station to highly controversial shellfish station (East Coast)—or from taco truck to dumpling truck to donut truck (West Coast)— in honor of turning thirteen; or calling the caterer for cutting a baby boy's foreskin; or receiving mounds of rugelach for dying is actually a legit Jewish thing. It's called a *seudat mitzvah*, which literally means "commanded meal," a festive, food-centric celebration meant to follow every life event.

So, good news, Jews, and those who eat like us: We are basically under obligation, by birthright, to pile our plates high.

Really, when you get down to it, a Jewish life is marked by meals. From bris to shivah and every major or makeshift occasion in between, we eat. Too much. Together.

L'Chaim

BRIS
The first slice

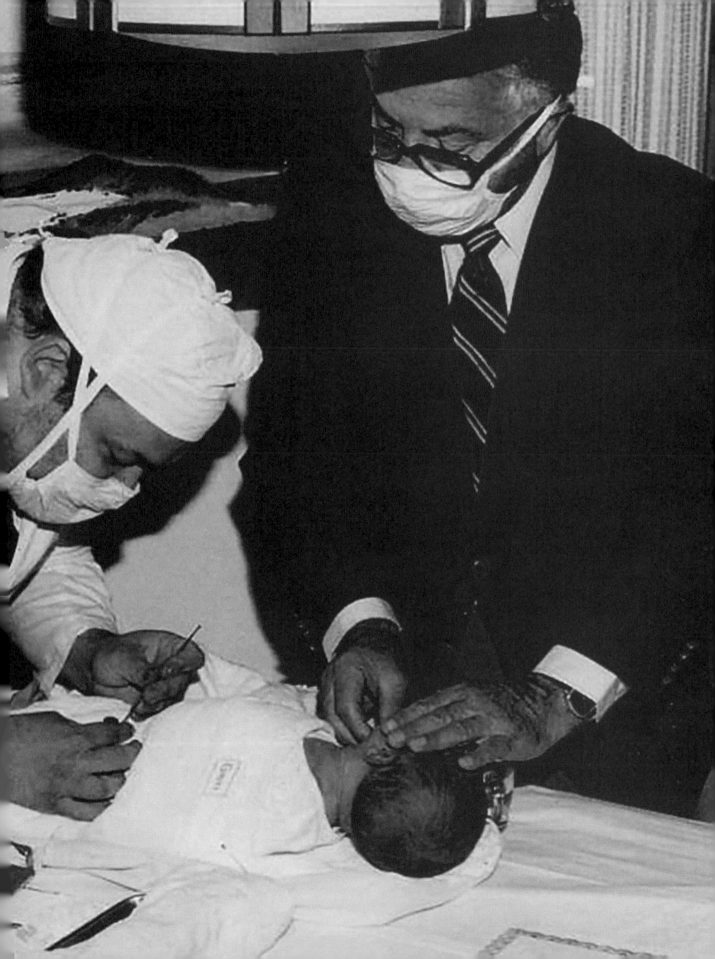

On Pastrami & Penises

Northern California's most prolific, and only full-time mohel, Moshe Trager, sums up every bris like this: "I say a few words, do my thing. It takes about fifteen seconds. We say Mazel, then eat some bagels." Like many West Coast Jews, and twenty-first-century Jews in general, I wasn't 100 percent sure I wanted to have a bris for my newborn son. My mother wanted me to. My mother-in-law wanted me to. My grandmother would've stopped asking me to visit her in Florida if I didn't. I mean, I wasn't going to snub four thousand years of tradition. (The practice is rooted in Genesis, where God instructs Abraham to circumcise himself and all of his descendants as a sign of their contract with God.) But I had a few reservations. Number One: I didn't have a signed contract with God. Also, the medical benefits of circumcision are only somewhat proven. I wasn't going to argue, though, with what's really an indisputable fact: A circumcised penis just, well, looks better. Still, the question remained: Must I throw a house party for it?

Then my friend Miranda, a San Francisco half-Jew, said, "But what if you had it catered!" Suddenly, a platter of house-smoked pastrami made the whole idea more palatable.

Indeed, catering the Cut is big business. This is especially true in the New York metropolitan area, where kosher companies with names like Ram Caterers and 8th Day and Foremost Caterers have been delivering bagel platters for *brit milah* (Hebrew for bris, which is Yiddish) for decades. Some new parents choose to host a simple affair at their synagogue, others opt to throw a 300-person, $200-a-head party at the Waldorf-Astoria, complete with a klezmer band and fully mic'd baby.

"Let's be honest, no one's there to see the show," says Evan, who doesn't remember his.

Trager agrees: "Very few guests actually watch the circumcision itself; they just mill about in another room, awaiting the after party." Moshe has all five-star reviews on Yelp. (Written by parents, of course—not the newborn boys themselves, or the reviews wouldn't be quite so raving.) Over the last quarter century, he has done more than 8,000 circumcisions on eight-day-old boys from Philly to Maui. That's nothing compared to New York's big-name mohels, he admits. And it pales in comparison to his mentor, back in Jerusalem, who racked up more than 100,000 circumcisions before he died and passed his booming business on to his son.

At 99 percent of the brises Trager does, bagels are served. But the Talmud actually commands us to serve meat—to ensure a rich life. "Bagels, in fact, have absolutely nothing to do with it," he explains. "Jews just like them, and they're convenient: easy to serve, easy to clean up." If you want to host a *proper* bris, he says, serve pastrami.

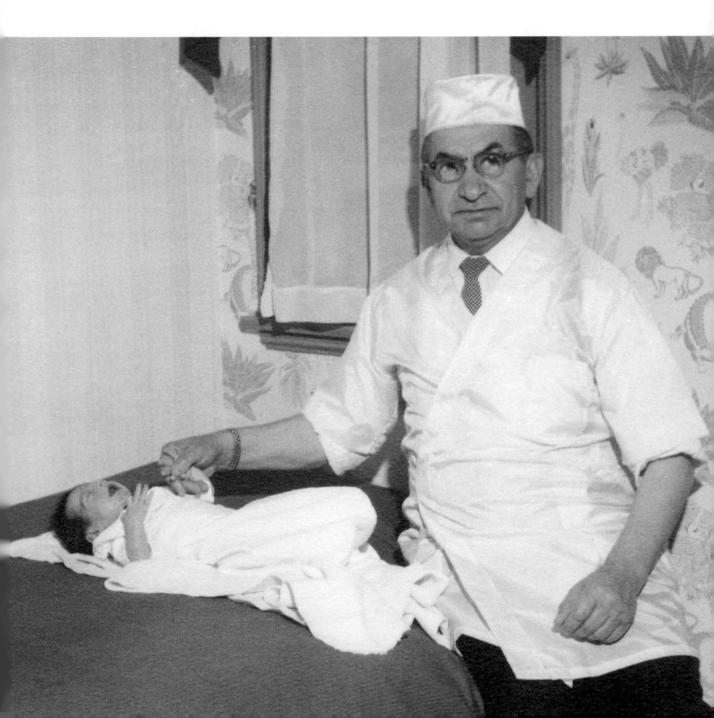

Leftover Pastrami All Day

Breakfast Tacos

Makes 6 tacos

Heat **2 Tbsp of any oil** in a large skillet over medium heat. Add **½ cup [75 g] of chopped onions** and sauté for 6 minutes. Add **2 cups [300 g] of chopped pastrami** (or corned beef or a combination) and **dashes of chili powder**, **garlic powder**, and **dried oregano**. Sauté for another 3 to 4 minutes. Transfer to a plate. In the same pan, scramble **4 eggs**. You know how. Heat **6 corn tortillas** directly over a gas burner on low to get that nice toasty taste. Top with the meat and eggs, and add **chopped avocado**, **hot sauce**, and anything else you like. While the new baby wails in the background, assume the proper position: Hover over the kitchen sink. Eat. Drip. Lick.

Pastrami Carbonara

Serves 2

Boil a large pot of salted water and add **8 oz [225 g] of pasta**, preferably spaghetti or another long noodle shape. While the pasta cooks to al dente, heat a large skillet over medium-high heat, and add **1 Tbsp of olive oil**, **1 whole garlic clove**, and **¼ cup [40 g] of chopped pastrami**. Cook until golden brown and crispy, 6 to 8 minutes. Set aside and keep warm. In a large bowl, whisk **4 egg yolks** well, and then fold in **¼ cup [25 g] of grated Parmesan cheese**. Drain the pasta, reserving about ¼ cup [60 ml] of the pasta water. Do not rinse. Add the drained, hot pasta to the bowl of eggs and cheese, tossing with two spoons or tongs. Speed is key here, to keep the egg from scrambling. Once combined, discard the garlic clove, and then add the pastrami bits, the oil from the pan, and the still-hot pasta water you've saved. Toss. Add a couple of grinds of **black pepper**, and keep tossing until the pasta glistens. Plate it, and top with more cheese and pepper. Grab a fork. Devour.

Raid-the-Fridge Reuben

Makes 1 sandwich

While you're heating up a big skillet over medium-high heat, whip up Russian dressing, using a **3:1 ratio of mayo to ketchup**, and add **salt and pepper**. (See the complete recipe on page 76.) Slather on **2 slices of bread** (your choice). On one of the slices, lay a slice or two of **any type of cheese**, and top with **sauerkraut**, **pickles**, or even **kimchi**. Set aside. The pan should be really hot by now. Toss in **1 Tbsp of neutral oil** and **1 cup [150 g] of sliced pastrami** (turkey and ham—God forbid—work, too). Cook for 1 minute on each side, adding more oil if needed. Leave the pan on the heat, but remove the meat and stack it up on the slice of bread with the cheese, etc. Put the second slice of bread on top, and transfer to the hot pan. Cook until the cheese is melted, about 2 minutes per side. Mmm.

Hanukkah
The second-class holiday

Christmas Inferiority Feelings, with Latkes

*Growing up Evan's mom gave him and his brother Hanukkah stockings. Like Christmas stockings, but baby blue, embroidered with "Evan" and "Ari"—and a menorah. Hanukkah stockings! Apparently, it's a thing.

It's inevitable. At some point in your young Jewish life, no matter how many gifts you opened or how many latkes you ate or how many bags of sparkly gold gelt you got—like most Jewish kids in America, like my kids last year—you asked for a Christmas tree. Maybe you felt a little left out of the mainstream. Maybe you wished you could sit on Santa's lap at the mall and hang hand-knit monogrammed stockings from your mantle.* And wander the streets belting out "Jingle Bells." And don matching outfits and pose for the most perfect family photo for the cards your mother sends out without a personal note to three hundred of her closest friends. And maybe, more than anything, you wished you could wake up in one-piece PJs super-early on Christmas morning and jump into a pile of presents as big as just-raked fall leaves, and spend hours under the tree unwrapping everything you ever wanted.

Those born into a fully assimilated or interfaith family might have had some of that. But most of us had Hanukkah. And how that worked was, after your parents got home from work on a Wednesday, after you ate leftover meat loaf for dinner, after you took a bath and did your homework, you got new days-of-the-week underwear. Granted, that was Night Five.

The first night of Hanukkah, however, is different. The first night is the most festive night of the Festival of Lights, when friends and family come over, when gifts are exchanged, when the menorah is lit—and that's kind of it.

Hanukkah is, at its core, a modest, minor league holiday. Its symbolic food is the humble potato, for crying out loud! Hanukkah is meant to commemorate the Maccabees' reclaiming of Jerusalem's Jewish temple after it was desecrated by Seleucid King Antiochus IV around 170 BCE. It honors the miracle oil that kept the temple's eternal flame flickering for eight nights, when it should have lasted only for one.

But, like so many things in life, Hanukkah, too, is all about timing. Had it been a summer holiday—who knows?—maybe it would've morphed into eight nights of fireworks, rather than the Christmas sidekick it's become.

One winter I spotted, in a Floridian's front yard, a ginormous "Hanukkah bear." A Michelin man–like blimp wearing a blue yarmulke, holding a massive dreidel in his Star-of-David-branded paws. Anchored to the manicured lawn, it was blowing gently—not in a breeze, but by an electric blower. Contemporary Hanukkah, it seems, has taken its cue not only from Christmas but also from car dealerships.

In the early nineteenth century, there were no blow-up bears or blue-and-white bulbs or brand-new bikes. In fact, there were no Hanukkah gifts at all. Just gelt. Not even the chocolate-covered kind. By the late 1800s, a bunch of Reform rabbis in Ohio had turned Hanukkah into a low-key kid party at the synagogue, with ice cream and oranges. It was sweet and simple and sort of festive.

Today, it's become a Christmas copycat. We've got Hanukkah movies and music videos from the Maccabeats. Tacky Hanukkah sweaters and Shark Tank hit toys like the Mensch on a Bench and its multimillion-dollar *mishpucha*: Ask Bubbe, Dreidel Dog, and Mitzvah Moose. The company's tagline: "To bring more funukkah to Hanukkah."

Hanukkah's commercialization is as much America's fault as it is the Jonesteins' desire to keep up with the Joneses, so to speak. It began as a way for immigrant Jews to demonstrate their economic success by buying presents for their kids, just like the gentiles did. Yiddish newspapers actually started generating revenue by running ads for gifts—the word "presents" was one of the first English words to appear in print.

Don't get us wrong. We don't mean to be a Scrooge. Presents are fun! Presents are good! Especially, as Jewish kids come to appreciate, eight nights of them. We're not advocating for a Hanukkah without gifts. Maybe just a Hanukkah without seven-foot-tall inflatable LED-lit lawn menorahs.

Ultimately, what makes a happy Hanukkah?

Really good latkes.

Latkes for All Eight Nights

Makes about 10 latkes

1 medium yellow onion, peeled and trimmed, with root end intact

1 lb [455 g] skin-on russet potatoes, scrubbed

2 large eggs, lightly beaten

¼ cup [45 g] potato starch

¾ tsp Diamond Crystal kosher salt

¼ tsp freshly ground black pepper

Vegetable oil for frying

1 bunch fresh chives, thinly sliced, for garnish

Our recipe guarantees ultra crispy latkes with a velvety interior. The smell of frying potatoes brings me right back to my grandmother's kitchen at Hanukkah. These are great as a side to brisket or any roast meat and perfect with smoked salmon for a decadent holiday brunch. If there are any left over, crisp them in a pan for a breakfast hash.

We have tried and tried to get the same texture using a food processor, and unfortunately, it's just not the same. A trusty box grater and a little knuckle blood are necessary for superlative latkes.

To keep the latkes warm until they're all cooked, preheat the oven to 200°F [95°C].

In a medium bowl, grate the onion on the large holes of a box grater and set aside.

Use the same grater (and holes) to shred the potatoes into a separate bowl. Wrap the grated potatoes in a clean kitchen towel or use your bare hands to squeeze out the water over a bowl or sink and discard the excess moisture. Make sure to squeeze out all of the water, so the potatoes brown well and don't steam too much in the pan; this will also reduce splattering. Work quickly once the potatoes have been grated to avoid discoloration. Transfer the potatoes to the bowl with the onion and fold together with a large spoon or spatula. Add the eggs, potato starch, salt, and pepper. Stir to combine.

Set a wire cooling rack over a rimmed baking sheet and line the rack with paper towels or paper bags.

Heat a medium cast-iron or other heavy-bottomed skillet over medium-high heat and add oil to a depth of ¼ in [6 mm]. When the oil is hot (about 360°F [180°C] on a candy or deep-fat thermometer), spoon about 2 Tbsp of batter per latke into the skillet, lightly spreading the batter into an evenly thick round. Don't overcrowd the pan. Cook, undisturbed, until golden brown and crisp on the bottom, 3 to 4 minutes. Carefully flip with a wide spatula and cook for 2 to 3 minutes more. You'll need to watch the temperature of the oil, being careful not to burn your latkes or, alternatively, end up with soggy and greasy clumps of potato if the oil is too cold.

Transfer the latkes to the paper towel–lined rack to drain, and season with another pinch of kosher salt. Repeat with the rest of the batter.

Garnish with chives and eat them hot, or keep warm in the oven while you cook the rest of the latkes. Latkes freeze particularly well in a resealable plastic bag. Reheat at 350°F [180°C] for about 15 minutes.

Salt matters. Diamond Crystal kosher salt is Wise Sons' go-to. While you can use other brands, or another type of salt, your recipes may not turn out the same because the crystal size, salinity, and weight will vary.

Lots of Kinds of Latkes

And no, we're not talking sweet potato. (Russet or bust, baby.) A few ideas for those times—like, say, Hanukkah's fourth through eighth nights—when you might tire of tradition.

Kimchi Latkes

Add to the batter a **few thinly sliced scallions**, **1 cup [about 130 g] strained, chopped kimchi**, and a **splash of soy sauce**. Cook the entire mixture as one big pancake in plenty of oil in a large nonstick or cast-iron skillet over medium heat, undisturbed, until golden brown and crispy, 4 to 5 minutes per side. Carefully flip using a large spatula. Garnish with **salt**, more scallions and **sesame seeds**.

Waffle-Iron Latkes

Add **1 more egg** to the batter. Place an even layer of batter in a well-oiled waffle maker and cook for 6 to 8 minutes, checking for a golden brown color. Repeat with the remaining batter. Season with **flaked sea salt** and serve with **soft-scrambled eggs**, **snipped chives**, and **smoked salmon**.

Masala Latkes

Add to the batter **heavy pinches of turmeric, garam masala**, and about **1 tsp of minced fresh ginger**. Cook according to the original recipe. Serve with **Greek yogurt** mixed with **lime juice**, **chopped fresh cilantro, salt**, and **mint**.

Make It a Latke Bar

You know, like a sundae bar, but for potato pancakes. Set out lots of toppings; here are some suggestions.

- Pickled Mustard Seeds (page 215), thinly sliced pastrami, and Horseradish Mayonnaise (page 49).

- Smoked Fish Salad (page 180); cherry tomatoes; and mint, parsley, and dill leaves dressed with lemon juice and salt.

- DIY Cured Fish (page 142) or smoked salmon, sour cream or crème fraîche, and thinly shaved fennel, cucumbers, and radishes.

- Soft-boiled eggs, caviar (tobiko or flying fish roe: cheap yet classy!), snipped chives, and flaky salt.

- Pickled Red Onions (page 215), sour cream, chopped fresh cilantro, shredded chicken or turkey, and habanero hot sauce, compliments of Wise Sons' Mayan chef, Manny.

- Shredded leftover Wise Sons' Brisket (page 167) and Rustic Applesauce (page 35).

Rustic Applesauce

Makes about 4 cups [960 g]

8 to 10 medium Golden Delicious or similar apples, peeled, cored, and cut into ¼ in [6 mm] cubes

⅓ cup [65 g] golden or dark brown sugar

2½ Tbsp apple cider vinegar

2 Tbsp fresh lemon juice

2 Tbsp unsalted butter (optional)

2 tsp Diamond Crystal kosher salt

½ tsp ground cinnamon

4 sprigs thyme

Combine all of the ingredients in a large heavy-bottomed saucepan over medium heat and stir to blend. Simmer for 25 minutes, scraping the sides and bottom of the pan constantly with a heatproof spatula to prevent burning or

Of all the apples out there, our pick for a rustic, chunky sauce is Golden Delicious—for its balance of sweetness and acidity. Add a few sprigs of fresh thyme for a savory layer and more complex flavor. A little brown sugar gives it rich caramelly notes. We like to add a tablespoon or two of unsalted butter during cooking, but that's optional.

sticking. If the applesauce starts to bubble and pop too much, lower the heat and add 2 Tbsp water to loosen the mixture. Be careful not to let the applesauce scorch or burn. You want all of the flavors to slowly caramelize. When the applesauce is finished, the diced apples should be softened but still hold their shape.

Remove from the heat and discard the thyme. If you like a smoother applesauce, purée in the pot with an immersion blender to the desired thickness. Spread out the applesauce evenly on a baking sheet to cool and prevent further cooking. Store in an airtight container in the refrigerator for up to 2 weeks, or freeze for up to 6 months.

The Battle of the Tree

According to a recent Pew survey, 32 percent of Jews had a Christmas tree in their home last year; 7 percent of those were Jewish couples, the rest were interfaith. For a lot of Jews in mixed marriages, the Christmas tree is a line they *will not cross.* Evan told his wife, before they married, that a life with him would have to be tree free. His brother, Ari, on the other hand, erects one every year. Some, like Jerry Seinfeld, compromise with, say, a Star of David at the top.

But for most mixed couples, it's an annual debate—one that my friend Wendy says goes something like this:

Gentile husband: This year, I'm buying a tree.

Jewish wife: Nope. I am not going to become one of those Jews who gets a tree on Christmas. We can eat cookies and go to parties and appreciate the glitter and glow from other peoples' windows, but we're not bringing one into our home. Plus, you have to admit, the whole tree hoopla is a bit much.

Gentile husband: You have no idea how important the tree is to kids! Buying it, decorating it, the morning under it, with all the presents! The tree made Christmas the best day of the year growing up. It will be the same for our daughter.

Jewish wife: Sorry, it's too religious to have a tree. No wreaths by the way, either.

Gentile husband: It's not religious! It's festive. I'll do it myself.

[Cut to]

Gentile husband drives to Whole Foods the day after Thanksgiving. He returns with the largest tree in the lot and shoves it into their tiny apartment. Daughter is excited. He strings up lights. The lights look pretty. They decorate. Fine, Jewish wife agrees, the tree smells nice.

Three weeks later, the tree dies and becomes an obvious fire hazard. Gentile husband brings it to the dump and Jewish wife sweeps up pine needles for days.

Twenty-four hours before Christmas, gentile husband goes back and buys a second, smaller tree. Daughter is excited. He strings up lights. The lights look pretty. They decorate. Jewish wife agrees the tree smells nice.

Then daughter asks if Santa Claus will come and Jewish wife says, without an ounce of Jewish guilt, No.

In Defense of Socks

We're not sure when socks became the lame-Hanukkah-present punchline, but it must have been back in the '50s, when boring white Hanes reigned.

In case you haven't noticed: Socks are cool now. It started with simple stripes and polka dots; now they've become high fashion. (The rapper Future spent $100,000 on Gucci socks to give to his girl, including several pairs of crystal-beaded knits, which cost $1,400 a pair.) But a cozy $10, $20, or even $30 pair from any one of dozens of hip sock sites will do.

"Me, personally, I was never great at gift-giving. Maybe it's because I never got to celebrate Christmas. I got Hanukkah. Doesn't exactly prepare you the same way. For Christmas, a gentile would get a bike, as a reminder that their parents love them. For Hanukkah, we would get socks, as a reminder that we were persecuted."

—Midge,
The Marvelous Mrs. Maisel

THE EARLY YEARS
PURIM

The Jewish Wonder Woman

Purim is a party. The Jewish Halloween, when kids run around the temple courtyard dressed up as Queen Esther and her adopted father, Mordecai, or Hermione and Han Solo, and wreak havoc with noisemakers.

Queen Esther is the star of the Purim cast. "Every woman relates to Queen Esther," says Rabbi Beth Singer of San Francisco's Temple Emanu-El.

What everybody loves about Purim, though, is an opportunity to eat hamantaschen, whether we actually like them or not. The triangular, fruit-filled cookies are said to symbolize Haman's pockets or his three-cornered hat or his ear, sliced off per medieval custom before hanging. But, as Rabbi Singer explains, "Some say the hamantaschen's vaginal shape, stuffed with poppy seeds, represents fertility and woman's empowerment." That works.

Hamantaschen
Better than you had in Hebrew School

Makes 30 cookies

One 16½ oz [470 g] store-bought sugar cookie dough

3 Tbsp vegetable oil

1 recipe Apricot Filling (page 227)

Crumble the dough into a big mixing bowl. Drizzle the vegetable oil over the dough, then, using your hands, mix until well combined. Divide the dough into two balls and press on them to make disks. Wrap in plastic wrap and refrigerate for about 1 hour.

Preheat the oven to 350°F [180°C]. Line a baking sheet with parchment paper. Roll out the dough on a well-floured work surface until about ⅛ in [3 mm] thick. Use more flour if you need—just don't let the dough stick!

Maybe you don't have time to make three dozen hamantaschen for your kid's class completely from scratch. In which case, store-bought dough will definitely do.

Using a 3 in [8 cm] round cutter, cut out as many rounds as you can and carefully place them on the prepared baking sheet. Ball up the remaining dough, roll it out, and cut more rounds. Repeat until you have used up all the dough.

Place about 1 tsp of filling in the middle of each round of dough. Fold three sides in, overlapping the corners to get a classic triangular hamantasch. Pinch the corners to seal and smooth any cracks. Repeat with the remaining dough and filling. Bake for about 15 minutes.

Variations

Prune

Substitute **prunes** for the dried apricots in the apricot filling.

Jam

In a small saucepan, whisk together **1 cup [300 g] of strawberry or raspberry jam** with **2 Tbsp cornstarch** over medium heat. Bring to a simmer, lower the heat, and simmer for 2 minutes. While the jam filling cools, roll out the pastry. Substitute the jam for the apricot filling.

Chocolate

Substitute **1 cup [180 g] mini semisweet chocolate chips** for the apricot filling. This one's extra easy and always a hit.

Poppy Seed

Combine **1 cup [140 g] ground poppy seeds**, **½ cup [120 ml] milk**, **¾ cup [255 g] honey**, **pinch of salt**, and maybe some **grated lemon zest** in a food processor; pulse into a coarse paste. Substitute the poppy-seed paste for the apricot filling.

Visiting the Grandparents in the Sunshine States

You have to go. You want to go.

"Eat Something"

Everyone knows: Schlepping to the Sunshine States to see your grandparents is as much of a Jewish tradition as eating Chinese food on Christmas (see page 79).

Evan went to Palm Springs. I went to West Palm. My kids now fly cross-country to Florida because my parents moved there. Evan's future kids may be spared this fate, as his parents "hate" Palm Springs. (Whether our kids' kids will have to winter somewhere warm and sunny with us remains to be seen; see page 228.)

As I once wrote in an essay for the *Wall Street Journal*, East Coast Jews have been making the trip for close to a century— so religiously, in fact, that the flight route between New York and Florida has garnered such nicknames as the Hebrew Highway, the Kosher Clipper, and our favorite, the Bagel Run.

Florida and Jews wasn't always a thing. But after the "No Jews. No Blacks. No Dogs." signs came down in the 1940s and the AC came on, the chain migration of snowbirds began. As seniors set south, they realized they liked palm trees and putting greens better than snow, and decided to stay. At least until spring. Today, South Florida is home to the country's third largest Jewish population (behind New York and LA), with hundreds of communities lining the multilane boulevards. Each offers the same lifestyle, if varying levels of luxury, behind every gate.

Be it Boca or Palm Springs or Sun City, Arizona, it's basically all the same: a time warp of a world with manicured greens and monogrammed golf carts; theme-night buffets and gendered card rooms; candy dishes and the clink of mah-jongg tiles; cul-de-sacs boasting exotic names like Tivoli and Marbella; and communal swimming pools— where we spent long, sweltering days under chlorinated water, timing our handstands and rating our dives, splashing and squealing, until, inevitably, an old man trying to swim laps would tell us to stop.

"Eat something," the grandmothers—always dry, always dressed—would urge from their chaises. The fancier kids would order lunch from the clubhouse. But Grandma Frances would drag us, still dripping, back to her apartment, where she'd slice up fat hunks of Hebrew National salami and stuff them between two slices of toasted rye, slathered with Gulden's mustard. Sans cheese, of course. A couple of Hydrox cookies for dessert, and it was back to the pool. Until dinner.

A Light Poolside Lunch

Evan's Dad's Sour Cream & Peaches

Makes 1 large jar

We don't serve this at Wise Sons, but I often eat sour cream and peaches at home. It's a Bloom men's tradition. After we kids had all gone to bed, my father would kick back in his armchair, read our two local newspapers cover to cover, and fix himself a snack—which always involved sour cream or cottage cheese and some sort of fresh fruit. (He had a subscription to the Harry & David Fruit-of-the-Month Club.) Dad's favorite treat was also a classic deli staple, typically done with canned peaches or apricots and likely marked on the large laminated menu with a little red heart, denoting "Healthy Choice." Which it is. I skip the Del Monte cans, of course. California!

For every **1 lb [455 g] of peeled, pitted, and sliced peaches** (about 3 medium peaches—commercially frozen are OK, too) use **1 cup [200 g] of sugar** and ¼ cup [60 ml] of water. Combine the ingredients in a saucepan over medium-low heat and cook, stirring occasionally, for about 15 minutes, until the syrup is medium thick. Cool, slice, and eat. Enjoy with **full-fat cottage cheese** or **sour cream**. Store in a glass mason jar in the refrigerator for up to 1 month or freeze forever.

Everything Dust Potato Chips

Makes 8½ oz [240 g]

Fact: French fries are fine, but potato chips are the absolute best side dish for a hot dog.

We doctor them, starting with a **large bag (about 8½ oz [240 g]) of kettle-cooked potato chips**—nostalgia calls for crinkle cut, if you can find them. Put about **4 parts Everything Spice** (page 92), **1 part nutritional yeast**, and a **pinch of brown sugar** in a coffee grinder and blitz until you have a fine powder. Set aside.

Spread out the chips on a rimmed baking sheet and bake for about 4 minutes in a 400°F [200°C] oven, tossing if you must halfway through. In a large bowl toss the warm chips with a tiny bit of **olive oil** and the Everything blend. For an herby pop your kids may or may not like, add a **handful of roughly chopped fresh dill**.

Cobb Salad

Makes 1 giant salad

A salad in name only, a true Cobb is a complete meal. A good Cobb has a solid mix of acid, umami, funk, crunch, and freshness—like this one.

Iceberg is the classic choice for lettuce, but we prefer a **hearty bowl of butter, leaf, romaine, and chicory**, tossed with **thin-sliced red onion**, a heavy squeeze of **fresh lemon**, a **splash of olive oil**, and some **kosher salt**. **Chopped turkey** is nice, along with creamy hunks of **avocado**, **hard-boiled egg**, and a **crumble of blue**, of course. But the key is **Crispy Pastrami** (page 49), a fitting substitute for that last bastion of *treyf*: bacon. In summer, **halved cherry tomatoes** are traditional, but fall and winter bring more creative options, like **roasted squash** and **diced tart apples**, or **pomegranates**. In spring, try **sugar snap peas**, **roasted asparagus**, and some **crispy shallots**. The final delicatessen touch: a few coins of **Pickled Carrots** (page 216).

Overheard in the Buffet Line

"Where did Josh go?"

"He's over there, staring at the desserts."

"Hello, hello. You're eating again?"

"Oh, Barry will eat again. Believe me."

"I can't love a good buffet any more than I do."

"I'm not even hungry and I'm going back for more. Why don't they give me a trough, and I'll get on my hands and knees?"

"I just don't know what to do: shrimp and grits or spaghetti and meatballs? Oh, I'll just get both."

The Club's Club Sandwich

Makes 1 sandwich

CRISPY PASTRAMI

Fatty pastrami, thinly sliced

SANDWICH

1 Tbsp unsalted butter, at room temperature, or vegetable oil

3 slices challah, homemade (page 125) or store bought

1½ Tbsp Horseradish Mayonnaise (recipe follows)

3 to 4 leaves crispy lettuce, such as iceberg or leaf

3 to 4 thin slices red onion

3 to 4 oz [85 to 110 g] roasted or smoked turkey, sliced

¼ ripe avocado, sliced

2 to 3 slices Crispy Pastrami

Potato chips, pickles, ketchup, and mustard for serving

To make the pastrami, preheat the oven to 350°F [180°C]. Lay the pastrami in one even layer on a foil- or parchment-lined baking sheet. Bake until the edges begin to crisp, about 8 minutes. Remove the pastrami from the pan and drain on paper towels until cool.

Store the pastrami, covered, in the refrigerator for up to 1 week. To serve, crisp up in a heavy-bottomed skillet over medium heat.

To make the sandwich, melt the butter in a large nonstick or cast-iron skillet over medium-low heat. Add the sliced bread to the pan (or work in batches, depending on the size of your pan) and cook until lightly browned and just starting to crisp on the bottom, about 3 minutes. Flip and cook for 2 minutes more.

A staple of both the classic American diner and the gated community golf club, the club sandwich is also a fixture on the Wise Sons menu. Griddling the bread makes for a superior sandwich than a standard toasted slice. Serve with tiny individual bottles of ketchup and mustard, if, like grandma, you've stolen them from that time you ordered room service.

Crispy pastrami is a classic Wise Sons' ingredient. It's a great stand-in for bacon—be it in this club, or an egg sandwich, or a peak-summer BLT, er, PLT.

Slather the tops of all of the bread slices with the Horseradish Mayonnaise. Top two of the slices with a few lettuce leaves and onion. Pile half the sliced turkey on top of each slice of lettuce-covered bread. Place all the sliced avocado on top of one of the turkey-covered bread slices, and the pastrami on the other.

Now, take the bread with the avocado layer and place it directly on top of the layer with pastrami. Take the last piece of bread, which should only have Horseradish Mayonnaise on it, and slap it on top, mayo-side down. Give the entire sandwich stack a smush with your palm. Use toothpicks to hold the sandwich together and cut into four triangles. Serve with potato chips, pickles, ketchup, and mustard.

Horseradish Mayonnaise

1 cup [240 g] mayonnaise

1 Tbsp store-bought, extra-hot horseradish

¾ tsp sugar

Mix the mayonnaise, horseradish, and sugar in a small bowl until combined. Horseradish Mayonnaise will keep in an airtight container in the refrigerator for up to 1 month. Makes about 1 cup [240 g].

We Found It in Grandma's Pocketbook

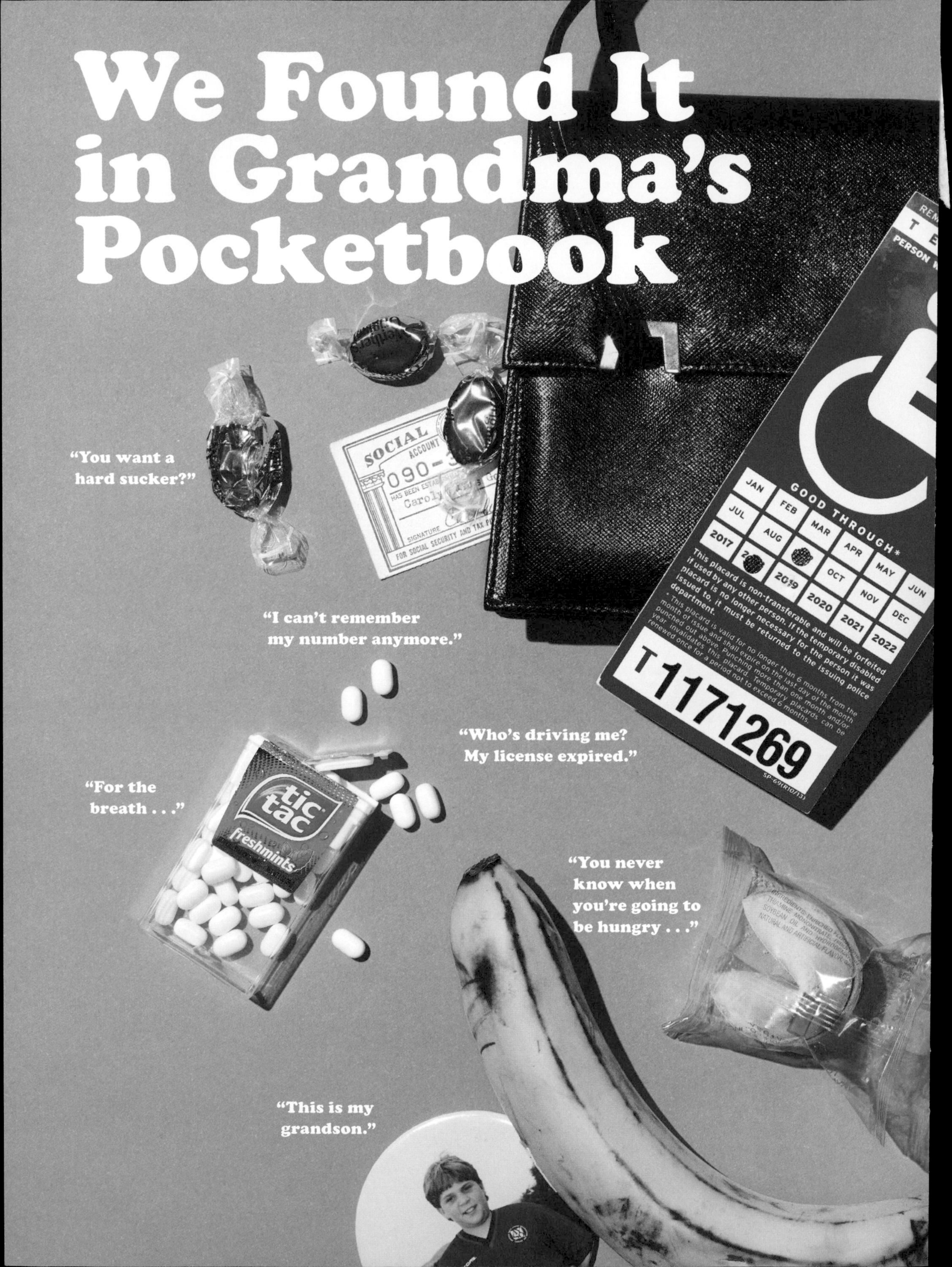

"You want a hard sucker?"

"I can't remember my number anymore."

"Who's driving me? My license expired."

"For the breath . . ."

"You never know when you're going to be hungry . . ."

"This is my grandson."

THE EARLY YEARS

SICK DAYS

It's called Jewish Penicillin for a reason

Nourishment for the Neurotic

Not to stereotype or anything, but those of us who know Jewish men or live with Jewish men or are parents of future Jewish men or are Jewish men will agree: They're not the best at being sick. (We're talking flulike symptoms, here.) It's a fate enforced by decades of both fictional (Alexander Portnoy, Ross Geller, Ray Ploshanksy) and real-life characters (Woody, Jerry, Larry). For better or worse, the archetype of the whiny, hypochondriac Ashkenazi male is alive and well! And what he needs—what we all need, these days—beyond love and attention and a lazy day on the couch watching Netflix, is chicken soup. Chicken soup as the soothing cure-all for the common cold, bad days, and breakups—for everything, really—is also a stereotype. For good reason: It's kind of true.

Jews have been slurping some sort of fowl soup since the twelfth century, when Sephardic physician-philosopher Moses Maimonides first prescribed it. (See "The Cure-All of the Twelfth Century," page 59.) Still, while Jews may lay claim to chicken soup, we certainly weren't the first to make it. The Chinese have been tossing domesticated birds and vegetables into clay pots for 10,000 years. Greek texts also touted its restorative properties, providing the basis for much of Maimonides's medical writings.

Twenty-first-century science has since gotten behind chicken soup, too. In 2000, a doctor at the University of Nebraska Medical Center named Stephen Rennard published a widely read study in the international medical journal *CHEST* supporting the anti-inflammatory benefits of chicken soup. Specifically, his wife's recipe, passed down by her Lithuanian grandmother.

Rennard found that homemade broth alone does bupkis, but adding vegetables like onions, carrots, celery, and parsley helped reduce flu symptoms and improve rehydration. Even pediatricians will tell you you're much better off cooking chicken soup for kids than force-feeding them over-the-counter cold meds.

OK, fine, it turned out Rennard's research found that canned commercial soup actually had similar inhibitory effects. But, whatever. We all know which one tastes better.

If there's one thing cultures across the globe have in common, it's a big steaming bowl of bird broth—whether it's a classic Jewish recipe or one infused with fish sauce or cumin.

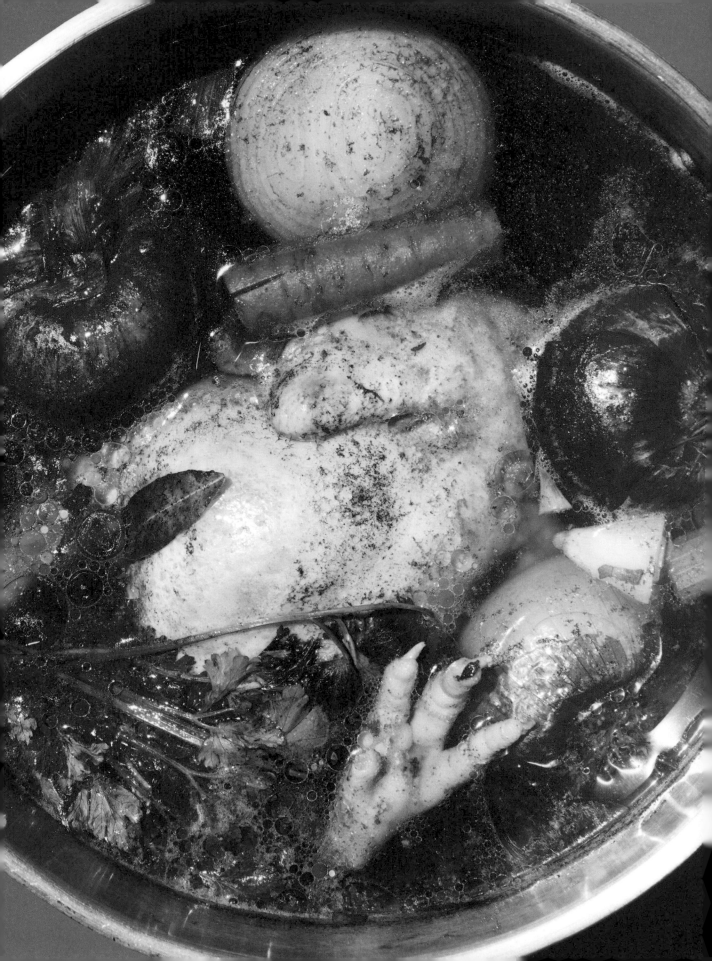

Wise Sons' Chicken Soup

Makes 4 qt [3.8 L] of soup and about 8 cups [1 kg] of shredded chicken

2 medium yellow onions, halved, with skin on

2 medium carrots, with peel left on, halved crosswise and split lengthwise

2 ribs celery, with leaves, quartered

1 Tbsp vegetable oil

One 4 to 5 lb [1.8 to 2.3 kg] whole chicken, giblets removed

¼ cup [10 g] sliced dried shiitake mushrooms

4 sprigs thyme

3 garlic cloves, peeled

2 dried bay leaves

¼ tsp black peppercorns

Diamond Crystal kosher salt

Matzo Balls (page 56), egg noodles, kasha, or rice for serving

Blanched carrot rounds (optional) for serving

Chopped fresh dill for garnish

We might be biased, but we think ours is the Chicken Soup of all Chicken Soups. Roasting the vegetables first creates a richer stock with a deeper flavor. It also contributes to a darker color, which we love. The mushrooms are our little secret, adding an umami boost to the finished product. If you can find them at your butcher, chicken backs and carcasses sub in well for a whole chicken and are more economical.

You could also do what we do at home: stash carcasses from your Friday roast chicken in the freezer, collecting them in a resealable plastic bag. A few chicken feet are always nice, too. Just drop them on top while the soup cooks to make it extra unctuous, just like Jews used to do in the old country. In addition to the carcasses, our home freezer is filled with containers of soup in various sizes, ready to go.

Preheat the oven to 400°F [200°C]. In a medium bowl, toss the onions, carrots, and celery with the vegetable oil to coat, then spread out on a rimmed baking sheet. Roast until browned, about 20 minutes.

In a large stockpot (with a capacity of about 16 qt [15 L]), combine the whole chicken, roasted vegetables, mushrooms, thyme, garlic, bay leaves, and peppercorns. Fill the pot with cold water, leaving only about 1 inch [2.5 cm] at the top. If your pot is larger, add more water.

Bring to a simmer over high heat, lower the heat to just above the lowest setting, and simmer gently for about 4 hours; you want the liquid to barely bubble.

Remove the pot from the heat and carefully take out the whole bird; it should fall apart quite easily. Set the chicken aside on a baking sheet or platter and let cool slightly, until you can handle the meat. Use your hands to pick all the meat from the bones, discarding the bones, skin, and cartilage. Put the picked chicken in a container and refrigerate.

With a slotted spoon or fine-mesh strainer, remove the largest vegetables and spices from the stockpot and discard. Strain the liquid into containers using a fine-mesh strainer or a colander lined with cheesecloth. Let cool and refrigerate overnight, then skim any fat that rises to the top with a spoon. Store, covered, in the refrigerator for up to 1 week, or in the freezer for up to 3 months.

To serve, bring the soup to a boil in a saucepan. Season with kosher salt. Add the cooked chicken, matzo balls, and blanched carrot rounds, if desired. Lower the heat and simmer until the chicken and matzo balls are hot. Serve garnished with fresh dill.

Matzo Balls

Makes 10 to 12 golf ball–size balls

4 large eggs

¼ cup [60 ml] Schmaltz (recipe follows), at room temperature (vegetable oil will do in a pinch)

1 cup [120 g] matzo meal, preferably Streit's

3 Tbsp Diamond Crystal kosher salt

⅛ tsp freshly ground black pepper

¼ cup [60 ml] seltzer water or club soda

Crack the eggs into a medium bowl and add the schmaltz. Using a whisk, beat the mixture until fluffy, about 1 minute. Slowly add the matzo meal, ¼ cup [30 g] at a time, using a rubber spatula to gently fold together and scrape down the sides. Add 1 Tbsp of the salt, the pepper, and the seltzer water. Gently combine. Cover the bowl with plastic wrap, and refrigerate for at least 1 hour, or up to 1 day, so the mixture firms ups.

Bring a large pot of water to a boil over high heat, and add the remaining 2 Tbsp of salt.

Meanwhile, remove the matzo ball batter from the refrigerator. Use a small scoop or spoon to scoop balls roughly the size of golf balls. Lightly oil your hands with vegetable oil. Roll each ball between your palms, forming it into a perfect round. Set the balls aside on a baking sheet.

Lower the heat under the pot of water to medium so the water is at a slow, rolling boil. Gently lower each matzo ball into the salted water. If you have it, a piece of parchment paper pressed against the surface of the water will help keep the matzo balls submerged, but it is not necessary. Place a lid on the pot and cook, undisturbed, for 30 minutes. Remove the matzo balls with a slotted spoon and serve immediately in chicken soup. Or shock in a bowl filled with ice and water to quickly cool. Drain and store in an airtight container in the refrigerator for up to 3 days.

A lot of bubbles, too many bubbles, make sinkers. We make floaters. Matzo balls are hard to get right—the steps are simple, but it's easy to mess up. Before we opened Wise Sons, we experimented with at least fifteen matzo ball recipes to find out how to make ultra-light ones. (But not too light!) Was the key baking powder? Or egg whites?

Ultimately we took the most basic recipe and doubled both the fat and the salt. One piece of advice for handling the matzo balls: It's a delicate batter, so easy does it. Like meatballs, try not to overwork it. No ginger or nutmeg or parsley necessary. Plop these in our chicken soup (page 55) and serve.

To reheat, add the matzo balls to a pot of soup, cover, and place over medium heat for 10 to 12 minutes, until warmed through.

 Streit's matzo meal is toastier and has a coarser texture than other brands we've tried. It's the only one we use. If you're making this for Passover, make sure the matzo meal is K for P (kosher for Passover).

Schmaltz

1 lb [455 g] chicken fat
1 medium yellow onion, thinly sliced

Place the fat and the onion in a medium heavy-bottomed saucepan over medium-low heat. Cook for 30 to 40 minutes, stirring every so often to prevent sticking, until the fat has completely melted, leaving crispy pieces of skin (gribenes), and the onions are a dark, golden brown.

Strain through a fine-mesh strainer and let cool completely. You can either discard or eat the onion and chicken skin left in the strainer. The schmaltz will keep in an airtight container in the refrigerator for up to 6 months. Makes about 1 cup [240 ml].

 Most butchers or high-end grocers should be able to sell you schmaltz if you ask. Try calling ahead so they can either save it for you while they butcher chickens or special-order it.

Leftover Chicken Broth
Three easy ways to doctor it up

Each makes enough to cure 2 hangovers.

Chicken Tortilla Soup

You probably have all of these ingredients on hand. A little leftover rotisserie chicken with chicken broth will give you a whole new meal.

Pour **4 cups [960 ml] of broth** into a small saucepan and add **1 cup [125 g]** or so of **shredded leftover chicken**. Add about **1 cup [240 ml] of your favorite tomato-based salsa**, **½ cup [80 g] of canned black beans**, **about 2 Tbsp frozen or canned corn**, and **2 tsp of ground cumin**. Bring to a simmer, and continue simmering for 20 minutes. Season with **salt**, **chili powder**, and more ground cumin to taste. You may also need to thin out the soup with a bit more broth or water, depending on your ingredients. Top with your favorite **hot sauce** and a **squeeze of lime**. Serve with **crushed tortilla chips**. **Cilantro leaves** and **sliced radish** and **scallions** are nice, if you've got them.

Pho Ga

Heat up about **4 cups [960 ml] of leftover chicken broth** in a small saucepan. Bring it to a simmer and season with a **few dashes of fish sauce** and a **pinch or two of sugar**. You want to barely taste the seasoning. Cover and keep hot on very low heat.

Cook **dried rice noodles** as directed on the package. Transfer to a soup bowl. Top with your favorite pho garnishes (**lime**, **chopped fresh cilantro**, **sliced scallion**, **chopped onion**, **sprouts**, **basil leaves**, **cooked chicken**). Pour the hot broth into your bowl. Finish with **hoisin** and **sriracha**; you know the drill.

Egg Drop Soup

Pour **4 cups [960 ml] of broth** into a small saucepan and bring to a low simmer. Toss in any **fast-cooking vegetables** you have handy (such as **cabbage**, **corn**, **celery**, **spinach**, **carrot**, **onion**, **snap peas**, or **bok choy**). Return the broth to a simmer and continue simmering until the vegetables are cooked. Stir the broth, and slowly pour in **2 beaten eggs** in a steady stream. Don't move your hand too much; you want to form some nice egg ribbons. Simmer until the eggs set, and then season with lots of **black pepper**, **sesame oil**, and **soy sauce**.

The Cure-All of the Twelfth Century

Soup made with fowl had some serious powers, according to philosopher-physician Maimonides (to be taken with a grain of salt).

TYPE OF SOUP	BENEFITS
Chicken	leprosy, emaciation
Turtle dove	poor memory
Partridge	constipation
Quail	kidney stone, poor urine flow
Duck	asthma
Pigeon	poorly regulated body heat
Chicken fat	frustration, anxiety, impotence

On the perfect size chicken for making chicken soup:

"One should not use the too large, that is of more than two years of age; nor the too small, that is those in whom the mucus still prevails; neither the too lean, nor those who through feeding become obese; but those that are fat by nature, without being stuffed."

—Maimonides,
in *The Medical Aphorisms of Moses Maimonides*

Mitzvah Moments

Professional dancers,
mountains of food, and more

Turning Thirteen Means Big Money

"My brother had a themed bar mitzvah before anyone was doing themed bar mitzvahs," says Irene Lax Boujo, a long-time LA event planner with Mindy Weiss Party Consultants. The year was 1969, and the theme was "Around the World." Every table was—you guessed it—a different country, with cut-out maps of Italy and Spain as centerpieces. It sounds so simple and handspun, almost quaint compared to today's bar and bat and nonbinary b'nei blowouts.

Today, some families literally take the party around the world. And we're not just talking Israel, which is a totally sensible, meaningful thing to do. But chartering yachts to the Caribbean, going on safari in the Serengeti, flying Bubbe and thirty thirteen-year-olds, sans parents, to a bimah in Buenos Aires? Renting out Radio City Music Hall or San Francisco's entire California Academy of Sciences to dance the hora with an African penguin colony? One friend recalls an especially over-the-top soiree at Gillette Stadium, where the parents partied with New England Patriots cheerleaders during cocktail hour, while the kids got a tour of the locker rooms. It's all been done in the name of newly ordained Jewish adulthood.

Hotel function rooms from Dix Hills to Beverly Hills are transformed every Saturday into serious tweenage ragers, with themes like Cooking, Cats, Candyland, or the Cohen-dashians. There are roving blackjack tables and sixteen-person foosball tables. Eponymous ice sculptures and body-length candy bars and never-ending slide shows. (Cue Taylor Swift's "Never Grow Up.") Always a prop-filled photo booth. And bags and bags and bags of swag, with monogrammed hoodies and trucker hats, sequin-studded sweats, and glitter socks marking the occasion forevermore.

"Does anyone really want to walk around with a tote that says 'Brad's Bar Mitzvah Bash, May 21, 2017'?" says Boujo. She advocates for more understated branding, which is where the newfangled logo comes in. "It used to be names—names on napkins, names on invites, names on *kippot*." Now every kid has a painstakingly designed logo, like she's a tech start-up. For example, my nephew's logo last year, after much debate: two black diamonds accompanied by the words "Experts Only." The theme, on Long Island in October, was skiing.

"The big thing in LA these days is hiring name entertainment," says Boujo. (For $250,000 per song.) Bruno Mars. Nick Jonas. Iggy Azalea. Aerosmith. Oh yeah? Well at *my* bat mitzvah, at the Crowne Plaza on Route 9, in Framingham, Massachusetts, we had, for reasons still unclear to me, a surprise Pee-wee Herman impersonator. Evan's was classier. He had a live swing band with Lindy Hoppers. He also wore a fedora.

Most, though, have DJs. DJs that come with party motivators paid to pump up the jam and lure shy tweenagers off their phones and onto the dance floor. These hard-bodied dancers are too old for a nice thirteen-year-old Jewish boy, like my nephew, to date (but apparently totally fine to flank,

in tight, midriff-baring tees and high-heeled thigh-high boots, as he makes his grand entrance). DJs, like Chicago's Kareem Wells, a.k.a. KWOE, a.k.a. #kingofthemitzvahs, a former West Side drug-dealer-turned-local-tween-icon with a three-year wait list who wouldn't be caught dead playing Kool & the Gang's "Celebration."

"Music is the Number One most important element to a successful party," explains Boujo. Number Two is physical comfort—no cold air or slow valets, overcrowded bars or long bathroom lines. That stuff matters. Coming in at Number Three, but still very important, of course: food.

"People have to feel like they've been given *enough* food," explains Boujo. "Otherwise our clients are afraid people will think they're being cheap." And no Jew wants to perpetuate stereotypes and be perceived as being cheap.

Quantity, it seems, matters more than quality, at least on the East Coast, where it's all about the

Stations. (See "Cocktail Hour at a Post-Modern Long Island Bar Mitzvah" on page 69.) "East Coast is major food," says Boujo. "Their cocktail hour, oh my God." The West Coast is more restrained. "We just don't eat like that out here," she says. LA has its own issue: "Women *won't* eat."

Maybe the Midwest is the happy medium? I called up my friend Dave, in Kansas, who had recently thrown his son a bar mitzvah. It was definitely more mellow than New York, where he grew up, he says. "For starters, we spent $7,000, not $70,000." No theme. No party planner. No party favors. No food stations. Just a good old Kansas-style barbecue, a DJ who played "Hava Nagila" on request, and a guest list comprised of mostly gentiles, who'd never been to a bar mitzvah before. "They had no idea how to hoist the chairs," says Dave, laughing. "I fell off. In the history of the hora, has anyone ever fallen off the chair?"

Crazy idea: What if we brought the bar and bat mitzvah bash down a notch? Back to the house, the backyard, the beach, even a bowling alley? At thirteen, the rapper Drake had his in the basement of an Italian restaurant. Even the "re–bar mitzvah" he threw himself at age thirty-one was a relatively low-key affair, with pizza and red Solo cups (albeit brimming with Perrier-Jouët Belle Epoque rosé).

What if we just make a massive pile of pigs in a blanket (all beef, of course), create a killer playlist, put up a life-size poster of our sweet tween in braces, and call it a post–haftorah portion party?

The mitzvah milestone won't be any less meaningful if we made it a little more about tikkun olam, and a little less about sequins and swag, and it might even be more so.

Although then we wouldn't have these pictures . . .

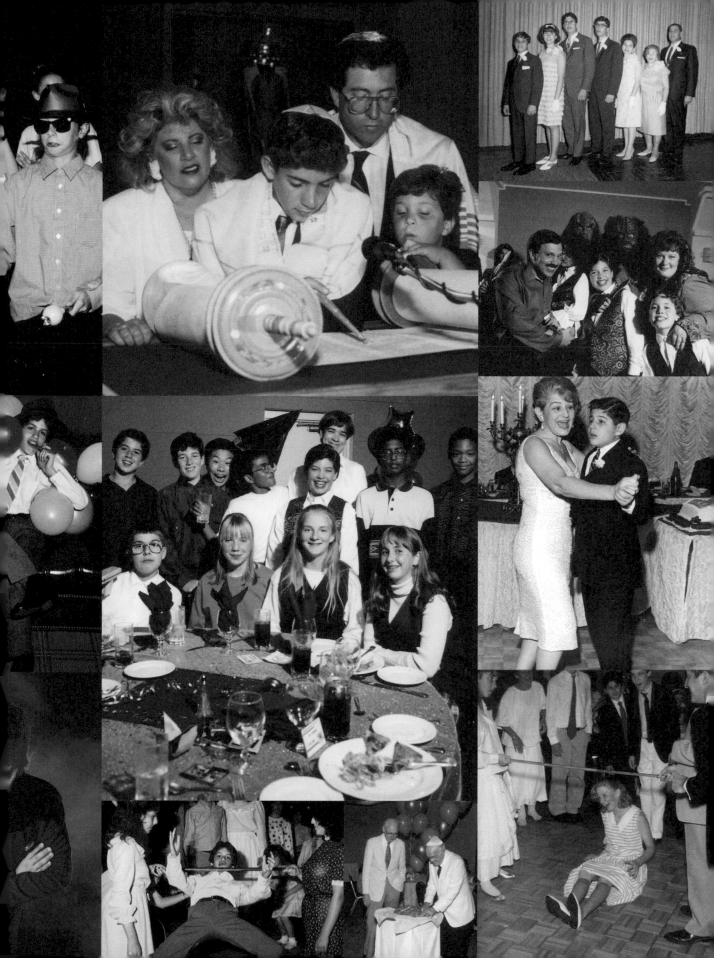

"Pigs" in Blankets

Makes 18 "pigs"

One 8 oz [225 g] tube Pillsbury crescent roll dough

One 12 oz [340 g] six-pack Hebrew National hot dogs, cut into thirds

Hebrew National hot dogs + Pillsbury crescent roll dough = true magic. "It's all anyone really wants," says party planner Irene Boujo.

Preheat the oven to 350°F [180°C]. Lightly grease two baking sheets with cooking spray.

Roll out the dough, and cut out the triangles. Cut each triangle into four smaller triangles. (Note: You will have leftover dough.) Wrap one triangle of dough around each of the minidogs. Place them on the prepared baking sheet, spaced at least 1 in [2.5 cm] apart. Bake until puffed, golden, and crisp, about 13 minutes, rotating the pan midway through baking. Serve immediately.

Other Things in Blankets

Okonomiyaki

After baking, top with **Kewpie Japanese mayo**, **katsu sauce**, and **bonito flakes** or **furikake**.

Southwest

Before baking, wrap a small piece of **pastrami** in the dough along with each dog. Brush **barbecue sauce** on top and continue with the recipe. Minutes before they are ready to come out of the oven, top with more sauce and some **grated Cheddar cheese**. Bake until the cheese is bubbly.

Lumpia

Instead of large franks, wrap minidogs in **wonton wrappers**. Deep-fry in vegetable oil until crispy. Serve with **Chinese hot mustard** and **sweet chili sauce**.

Breakfast

Use **breakfast sausage links** instead of hot dogs. Serve with a sauce made of equal parts **maple syrup** and **whole-grain mustard**.

Philly

Sauté **sliced onions** and **peppers** until tender. Split open the top of each baked pig in a blanket and smother with the onions and peppers. Top with **shredded cheese**.

Peking

If you can find **duck sausage**, use that, but the classic Hebrew National will work, too. Using a **Chinese steamed bun**, stuff with a cooked sausage or hot dog, a shmear of **hoisin**, sliced **cucumber**, and **cilantro**. Top with crackly **chicken skin** if you have it.

Hawaiian

Cut **leftover corned beef** into little logs, and brush with **teriyaki sauce**. Wrap in **crescent dough** and sprinkle **furikake** on top. Bake as directed in the recipe and top with a piece of **pineapple**. Aloha!

Cocktail Hour at a Post-Modern Long Island Bar Mitzvah

Food Stations:

Sushi boats

Mac 'n' cheese bar

Mashed potato bar, with all the toppings

Cheese, crackers, and crudités

Chopped liver and Nova

Bacon bar: applewood, smoked,
and pepper crusted, on sticks (controversial)

Sliders

Brisket and corned beef carving station

Garnish-your-own Bloody Marys

Plus, the passed apps:

Smoked salmon pinwheels

Mac 'n' cheese bites

Kobe sliders

Tuna tartare cones

Spring rolls

Chicken skewers

Beef satay

Lamb chop popsicles

Franks en croûte (that's French for pigs in blankets)

Signature cocktail: a blue raspberry martini

"I went to twelve bar and bat mitzvahs this season. I'm a professional guest. There was one where the food was served family style. AND THERE WASN'T ENOUGH. Worst faux pas ever. People were battling forks and scraping platters. Everyone is still talking about it."

—A Jewish mom from New Jersey

The above cocktail-hour feast was followed by a three-course, sit-down supper, including a bread basket and dessert, with four full-size sweet treats per plate.

Tweenagers Review Their Favorite Bar & Bat Mitzvahs

San Francisco, CA

"It was at the Academy of Sciences. We had the whole museum to ourselves, with a red carpet leading in. They had really good snacks, like boba tea and giant vats of candy. And henna and personalized sweatshirts, and we could make replicas of our hands with colored wax—and everyone got a cow onesie!"

—*Dylan*

Scarsdale, NY

"The theme was Tesla. We got to race cars around a small track. (Those weren't Teslas, though.) Everyone got a remote control car to take home. They had DJs and professional dancers, so I just danced the whole time. I didn't even eat! But for the kids, it's always french fries, mac 'n' cheese, and chicken fingers. The coolest moment was the bar mitzvah boy's grand entrance: He drove in on a golf cart."

—*Amanda*

Oakland, CA

"It was a casino theme. They had blackjack and roulette. Classic arcade games, too. The food was good: salmon sliders, latkes, grilled asparagus, these beef skewer things, and s'mores and strawberries. And my dad said the wine was selected by a sommelier from Chez Panisse."

—*Scarlett*

Waltham, MA

"My favorite bat mitzvah was mine! I thought about a theme—rainbows, tie-dye, books—but it wasn't for me. I just wanted to show up and dance: the Cupid Shuffle, the Electric Slide, Cotton Eye Joe. Even my older sister and her moody friends got on the dance floor for the Macarena. I was wearing a sleeveless dress and got supersweaty, which got kind of awkward during the trust falls."

—*Isa*

Tenafly, NJ

"I go to at least one bar or bat mitzvah every weekend. The best so far was the one at MetLife Stadium. The theme was football. It was on the field. We all got pajamas with our friend's initials on them, and they had fried Brie. I got in trouble for taking too many."

—*Axel*

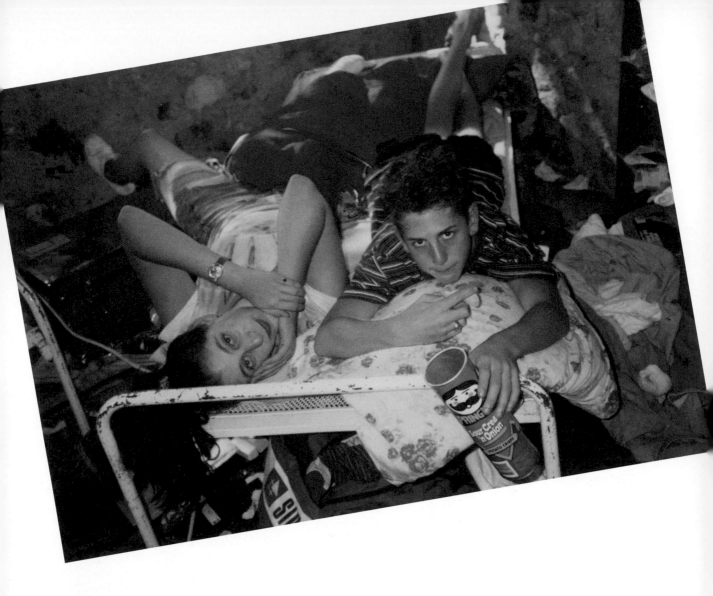

The Last Supper

'Twas the night before summer camp . . .

Cheeseburger Time

Camp food! Unless it's grilled cheese or Chipwich day, it's rarely good. It's also, at most Jewish sleepaway camps, kosher style. So no bacon or pulled pork, no shrimp poppers or pepperoni pizza. And above all, to most kids' chagrin, no cheeseburgers.

Which means the Night Before Camp is kind of a big deal, as far as dinner is concerned. A "last supper" decision akin to that always-fun hypothetical question: "What would you want your final meal to be before you die?" Except instead, it's before you go away for two or four or eight weeks, to canoe and play tennis and maybe make out for the first time.

Some LA kids might select sushi. Gaggles of girls in New York might gather for frozen yogurt. And according to one New England father, "The entire week leading up to camp has been declared the Week of Eating Everything We Won't Be Able To." He explains, "One night fajitas, the next pork chops, then shrimp cocktails, and then Thai."

But for most kids, there is no contest. East Coasters convene at Five Guys. West Coasters head out to In-N-Out, like Evan and his friends used to do before shipping off to Camp Alonim. In Wisconsin, before a summer at Camp Interlaken, Kopp's is always swarmed. Growing up in suburban Boston before the "good chains" came along, I had the existential choice between McDonald's or Burger King. (Flame-broil all the way.)

But behold Wise Sons' Big Macher. After packing, why not stay home and make your own.

Big Macher Burger

Makes 4 burgers

4 oz [115 g] pastrami

1 lb [455 g] 80/20 ground beef
(80 percent lean beef and 20 percent fat)

1 Tbsp vegetable oil

4 tsp Diamond Crystal kosher salt

4 slices American cheese
(or Cheddar, if you must)

4 sesame seed challah buns

¼ cup [60 ml] Russian Dressing (page 76)

16 Pickled Cucumbers Bread & Butter Style (page 215)

¼ cup [40 g] chopped yellow onion

2 cups [150 g] shredded iceberg lettuce

Full sour dill pickle spears for serving

Our spin on the classic diner burger. Pastrami scraps mixed into the beef blend gives it a unique smoky flavor. Visiting my grandparents in LA, I frequented Pico Kosher Deli, where my go-to order was a burger topped with sliced hot pastrami. It was the inspiration behind this burger, which has become one of Wise Sons' signature dishes.

Finely chop the pastrami or pulse quickly with a food processor, taking care not to overprocess, which will heat the meat. In a large bowl, combine the ground beef and chopped pastrami. Use clean hands to mix the meats together until well combined, but do not overmix. Use a kitchen scale to weigh out four 5 oz [140 g] portions or simply eyeball them, forming each into a smooth round ball between your palms. Gently press each patty into a flat puck, tossing and patting between your hands until you have a nice flattened patty, about 5 in [12 cm] across and ½ in [12 mm] thick. Transfer to a large plate, cover with plastic wrap, and refrigerate until ready to cook. The patties can be made up to 1 day in advance.

Set a large cast-iron skillet over medium-high heat and coat evenly with the oil. When the oil is shimmering, remove the patties from the refrigerator and sprinkle the tops liberally with half the salt; flip, and sprinkle with the remaining salt. Add two patties to the pan, and cook until a light brown crust forms on the bottom and the burger is turning from pink to brown at the edges, about 3 minutes. Carefully flip with a spatula, and place a cheese slice over each burger. Cook for 2 minutes more for a medium-rare to medium burger. The cheese will have melted well at this point. Transfer

continued

the cooked burgers to a plate or baking sheet. Repeat with the remaining patties.

With the oil and beef fat still in the pan, place the buns, cut-side down, in the pan and cook over medium-high heat for 2 to 3 minutes, until a golden, toasty crust has formed. Flip and cook for 1 minute more to heat the buns completely.

Put a heaping spoonful of dressing on the bottom half of the bun, spreading it out to the edges. Spread out four bread and butter pickle coins on top, and sprinkle with onion. Place the cheese-covered patty on top, and cover with a heap of lettuce. Spread a bit more dressing on the top bun to "glue" it to the burger toppings, and use your palm to gently smush everything down. Serve with a sour pickle spear.

Russian Dressing

½ cup [120 g] mayonnaise

1½ Tbsp ketchup

**1½ Tbsp grated yellow onion
(use the small holes of a box grater)**

1 Tbsp dill pickle relish

½ tsp Worcestershire sauce

½ tsp sriracha

Pinch of garlic powder

Freshly ground black pepper

In a small bowl, whisk together the mayonnaise, ketchup, onion, relish, Worcestershire, sriracha, garlic powder, and a few grinds of pepper until well combined. Store, covered, in an airtight container in the refrigerator for up to 1 month. Makes about ¾ cup [180 ml].

On Care Packages: Disguising Camp Contraband

Outside food is rarely allowed at summer camp. And yet, every summer, parents around the country go to impressive lengths to try to smuggle snacks to their not-starving offspring. A few popular ploys:*

- Eviscerated teddy bears restuffed with jelly beans
- Flashlights filled with Sour Patch Kids in lieu of batteries
- Smarties tucked into tampon boxes
- Cans of Pringles inside cans of tennis balls
- Pixie Stix taped perfectly flat inside birthday cards
- Sticks of gum neatly inserted inside cartons of Band-Aids (inside the actual Band-Aid wrappers)
- Tubes of toothpaste with the toothpaste taken out, Twix put in, and the two halves of the tube glued back together.

All failed attempts, except the Pixie Stix birthday card.

Campers weren't allowed Fritos or Cheetos or Mom's chocolate chip cookies. But every Friday night, every kid age seven and up got a Dixie cup of Manischewitz. The older kids would go around stealing the younger kids' until their own cups were overflowing. And always, a bottle would mysteriously go missing from the stash in the kitchen.

"My father once mailed me a 5-gallon jar of Guss's pickles (full sours), direct from the Lower East Side. Bold move. He did not try to hide it. I talked my way into keeping the tub of (ahem, kosher) pickles, as long as I shared."
                                        —A former camper

Christmas Dinner

An ancient Jewish tradition

Can We Get A Lazy Susan Topped-Table for Twelve, Please?

The first record of Jews eating Chinese food on December 25 dates back to 1935. "Yule Stirs Chinese to Aid Jewish Home" read the *New York Times* headline. A restaurant owner in Newark, New Jersey, by the name of Eng Shee Chuck, brought chow mein for eighty, along with toys wrapped in red ribbon, to a Jewish Children's Home. They ate and talked and told stories. "It was a wonderful Christmas," he'd told the *Times*.

And, lo, a new Jewish tradition was born. A tradition that now comes with annual, sold-out Christmas Eve dinner shows like Moo Shu Jew in Philadelphia and Kung Pao Comedy in San Francisco. A tradition highlighted in scholarly books like *A Kosher Christmas: 'Tis the Season to Be Jewish* by Rabbi Joshua Eli Plaut (2012). A tradition essentially codified by U.S. Supreme Court justice Elena Kagan when, at her confirmation hearing in 2010, Senator Lindsey Graham asked what she was doing one Christmas, and she famously replied: "You know, like a good Jew, I was probably at a Chinese restaurant." The Senate erupted in laughter, on both sides of the aisle. It's a tradition that has officially morphed into a meme, yes. But it's also a tradition, few realize, that's rooted in real meaning.

This holiday season, as you join Jews across America in slurping egg drop soup and shoveling xiao long bao, take a moment to consider why. Why, on Christmas night, do we eat Chinese food?

Because in the late nineteenth and early twentieth centuries, the Jews and Chinese were both outsiders, as Jennifer 8. Lee, producer of *The Search for General Tso*, explains. As the two largest non-Christian immigrant groups in New York City, they shared a feeling of otherness—as well as a "fence," since the Lower East Side's Jewish tenements bordered Chinatown.

Because Chinese restaurants let Jews in. Because Chinese restaurants weren't decorated with crucifixes and depictions of Jesus, like the Italian restaurants. Because Chinese restaurants offered a dairy-free gateway to treyf. Because wontons and kreplach were basically one and the same. Because Chinese restaurants were affordable. And cosmopolitan. And, well, because Chinese restaurants were open.

Today, Chinese restaurants in America brace for the big day. People book reservations months, if not a year, in advance. The restaurants bring in additional bussers. Every server on payroll is on the floor.

The half-century-old Shun Lee Palace in Manhattan does some 1,300 reservations every Christmas Day. On a typical night, Ed Schoenfeld serves about 450 diners combined at his three modest-size, modern Chinese restaurants in Manhattan. On Christmas, the total number of diners served balloons to 1,200.

"It wasn't like this when I was growing up in New York in the '50s and '60s," he said. "Jews might have gone out for Chinese food because they didn't go to church, but it wasn't a thing, like it is now." And it's still a decidedly Jewish American thing. The tradition has yet to jump across the pond. Apparently, in the UK, Jewish families tend to do a turkey Christmas Day lunch and then, as one Brit told me, "watch the Queen's speech on TV at 3:00 p.m. precisely."

Christmas Day Confessions

From a Chinese restaurant guy:

"I started working at Golden Temple in 1979. I was in high school and my friend said, 'Hey, want to come wash dishes at this Chinese restaurant?' So I did. When I went off to college, I came back every Christmas break. They needed me. Then it turned into a summer job. After graduation, they offered me full-time as a host. And that was that. I've been here ever since.

"We were cash only, up until the '80s, when people started flashing credit cards. Sundays were always busier than the weekends. It was a whole bunch of Jewish families: the owners of the liquor companies and their wives, the Jewish bookies who'd line up at the pay phones to place bets for Sunday football. They've all either died off or were incarcerated.

"Today, I've got customers I met when they were eight, who are now forty-eight! We've got a ton of snowbirds, too. They call up and say, 'We can't find good Chinese food in Florida.' Or LA or Michigan. They miss our shrimp in lobster sauce and ask us to FedEx it to them overnight. It's like a $200 delivery fee. They don't care. They just want their lobster sauce. It's crazy.

"But Christmas is crazier. A lot of people say, 'Put me down for next year!' on their way out. I start getting calls around Halloween: 'Can I get a table for ten?' About 99 percent of Christmas reservations show up, so don't even try walking in on December 25. By 11 a.m., it's going gangbusters, until we close at 2:00 a.m. We've got 235 seats, and the bar, which is always packed, and the DJ lounge. We turn tables five, six times. So we serve 1,000 people, easy, on Christmas. Probably more. Plus takeout. Eventually we stop picking up the phone. From what I hear, at least. I'm a preacher's kid. I don't work Christmas."

—**Eric Hornfeldt,
General Manager of Golden
Temple in Brookline, MA**

From a deli guy:

"I'd never met anyone Jewish before. Now my life is devoted to making brisket and chopped liver and latkes. Thousands and thousands of latkes! At least 16,000 last Hanukkah. We do about 3,500 matzo balls on Passover. I could never pronounce 'matzo balls,' so I used to call them *albondigas de galletas*.

"I'm Catholic, from Mexico. I moved to San Francisco in 1999. My first job was washing dishes at a taqueria. Later, I was poaching eggs at a brunch place when my friend asked me if I wanted to come work for a new place called Wise Sons. I started as a line cook—six years later, now I'm the commissary manager and chef.

"Most nights, I bring leftover brisket home to my family. And babka. My family loves babka.

"I love pickled herring. Gefilte fish, too. I remember being up to my elbows in it with no idea what it was!

"It's different working at a Jewish restaurant. At other places, the menu changes with the season, or the chef's mood; there are new dishes all the time. Occasionally we'll have specials—like the trout salad melt. Mmm. But otherwise, it's the same every day. That's deli. It's tradition.

"We're always busy, but Christmas Day is crazy. Always a line out the door. I'm usually at the commissary by 6:00 a.m., setting up the kitchen, managing the bagel bakers, making sure no one slept in. People are always late on Christmas morning; I understand.

"For some reason, we get the most complaints on Christmas. Someone has to wait for a table or wait for their food. People don't like to wait. What else do they have to do on Christmas?

"At the end of the long day, Rodrigo usually brings in tamales, we'll get a turkey, and have a staff dinner together. Sometimes I'll make everyone brisket tacos or corned beef fried rice. I'm always adding habaneros, pickled onions, and lime to the chicken soup, to the latkes, to everything. Did you know matzo tastes great dipped in salsa?

"My brother works for Wise Sons. My sister does, too. She actually married one of the cooks at the Jewish Museum. A couple of my cousins are bakers. We're all one big mishpucha."

—Manny Interian, chef at Wise Sons

A Sampling of Iconic Chinese Restaurants, as Chosen by the Chosen People

New York City: Shun Lee West

Owner Michael Tong once estimated that about 70 percent of his clientele is Jewish. It's a Christmas tradition, he told the *New York Times*—for those who haven't gone to Florida or the Caribbean. For legions of New Yorkers, a weekly one, too. "Shun Lee's shrimp and lobster sauce is essentially kosher," joked one regular.

Los Angeles: Twin Dragon

Serving tiki cocktails and seafood fantasies to undiscerning Jews on Pico Boulevard's "Kosher Corridor" for almost sixty years. "Best mai tais in LA," Yelped "Lew S. from LA," who proudly touts he has been going for thirty-five years.

Pittsburgh: China Palace

Serving General Tso's chicken since 1988. Owner Mike Chen is the emperor of Chinese restaurants in Pittsburgh, and no matter how many new, regional, less-Americanized spots he opens—he's up to about a dozen by now—local Jews remain true to their roots: They go to China Palace, in Monroeville, where the wait is so long, lifers know: Pick-up is the only way to go.

St. Louis: Shu Feng

"You have to order the sesame chicken," one high school senior told the *STL Jewish Light* in an article entitled, "Top 10 Places to Spend Christmas." Eight of the ten places were Chinese restaurants. The others: a movie theater, of course (the AMC, where "all you have to do is press a buzzer and they bring you food!" he wrote) and the ice skating rink (*Steinberg* Rink. Coincidence?).

San Francisco: San Tung

It's not in Chinatown or on Clement Street, San Francisco's "other Chinatown"; it's not famous like Yank Sing, and it's certainly not rubbing chopsticks with Mr. Jiu's, but thirty-year-old San Tung is consistently swarmed with members of San Francisco's Chinese American and Jewish communities, with college students and tipped-off tourists. Everyone piles in for dumplings and dried fried chicken. Even at 4:00 p.m. on a Monday, San Tung's 100 seats are taken. Manager Frank Chu has been making dumplings here, alongside his mom—Mrs. Chu—since he was a teenager. "I don't get it," he once said to me, surveying the motley crowd. "If they eat now, do they still eat dinner?"

Chicago: Yu Lin Chinese Dumpling House

"Yu Lin was a friend of my grandfather's," recalls my friend Peter. "He was a banker in the next town over. I think he granted her a loan or something. She loved him. The place was big, almost cavernous. A barn of Chinese food. Huge plates, enormous helpings. We'd go on Friday nights. It was in a strange location, behind the police station, across from the Toys "R" Us. I always felt a little sick after, not because of the food but because I'd eat too much. And Yu Lin, a small lady with kind of big bouffant hair, she sort of looked like Annette Funicello. Very kind, laughing, would hover around us, saying to my grandfather, 'Seymour, Seymour, you're here!'"

Tulsa: New Royal Dragon

Tulsa's 2,500 Jews have been flocking to Royal Dragon for Yangzhou fried rice for forty years, and not only for its "Dreidels and Dumplings" day. "The food was quite mediocre, but it was the place to be," recalls one Oklahoma native. "There was a koi pond, and my mom always worried that my sister and I would fall in." Today, gone is the all-you-can-eat buffet and the 250-seat dining room—and the koi pond. Shuzhen Lin and her husband, Junlian Zhang, downsized to a smaller space, adding "new" to the name but still serving old favorites.

Miami: Tropical Chinese

"My grandma and I had a standing Friday night date for dim sum, and probably pork," recalls one Floridian. "The dim sum push cart was very exciting, too. Although the ones I loved never seemed to come around until I was too full. I'd get the sesame balls no matter when they passed by. Because, what if they don't come back? Scarcity issues and all."

The award for the Best Jewish-Named Chinese Restaurant in America goes to . . . Genghis Cohen, in LA, unseating Brooklyn's now-shuttered Shang-Chai.

Sunday Night Takeout

On the Jewish-Chinese bond

It's Like Every Week Is Christmas

Although Christmas is the day Jews celebrate Chinese food (see page 79), it is Sunday—as in, every Sunday—when we simply eat it, with friends and family. In front of the TV and without fanfare. Well, unless you count the chaos of ordering.

Be it by phone or online, there are always questions from the peanut gallery, including:

"Does the Kung Pao chicken have peanuts?" (Yes.)
"Do the dumplings have pork in them?" (Yes.)
"Will the Szechuan beef be spicy?" (Yes.)

As well as threats and demands:

"I won't eat scallops." (I know.)
"Get a shrimp dish!" (OK.)
"Make sure you order enough rice." (OK.)
"Ask them how long it will take!" (Too long.)

And, of course, the collective concern:

"Did we order enough food?" (We did.)

Jews in America have been eating Chinese food—a lot of Chinese food—since the late nineteenth century. In 1899, one Yiddish newspaper criticized the Lower East Side's Jewish community for flocking to nonkosher restaurants like the Chinese restaurants in the neighborhood next door. In 1928, another Yiddish paper decried Jews' slippery slope toward assimilation: "Down with Chop Suey! Long Live Gefilte Fish!" (Chop suey, of course, was itself a symbol of Chinese assimilation.) The author of that long-ago article would be pleased to know that today, gefilte fish has not only outlived chop suey, it's kind of having a moment.

Next Sunday night, instead of waiting forever for delivery, with its hefty fees and leaky containers, try cooking your own.

We know. Shanghai Dumpling King is delicious. But so are these recipes.

Cold Takeout-Style Noodles

Serves 4

¼ cup [60 ml] soy sauce

2 Tbsp toasted sesame oil

2 Tbsp distilled white vinegar

2 Tbsp smooth peanut butter
(the commercial stuff)

1 Tbsp golden or dark brown sugar
(white sugar will do)

1 Tbsp minced fresh ginger

1 Tbsp minced garlic (optional)

1 lb [455 g] fresh Chinese egg noodles or
ramen noodles, or even dried spaghetti

Shredded cooked chicken (page 55), julienned
cucumber, fresh cilantro leaves, toasted sesame
seeds, thinly sliced scallions (green parts only),
and Everything Spice Crunchy Chili Oil (page 92)
for garnish (optional)

Even when there's nothing in the refrigerator, there's always enough for sesame noodles—soothing in the winter, cooling in the summer, and cozy on a Sunday night.

In a medium bowl, whisk together the soy sauce, sesame oil, white vinegar, peanut butter, brown sugar, ginger, and garlic until smooth and the sugar is dissolved. Set aside.

Fill a large pot, bowl, or container with ice and half as much water. Cook the noodles until al dente, drain in a colander, and pour the noodles directly into the ice bath, shocking them to stop the cooking. Return to the colander to drain again.

Transfer the noodles to a large bowl, add the sauce, and mix well to combine. If desired, garnish with the chicken, cucumber, cilantro, sesame seeds, scallions, and Everything Spice Crunchy Chili Oil, and enjoy immediately.

 Fresh garlic adds a nice kick, but it's not mandatory. Use the best-quality sesame oil you've got and make sure it's toasted.

Whitefish Toast

Serves 10 (as an appetizer)

4 oz [115 g] boneless hot-smoked fish,
such as whitefish, trout, or even salmon

2 large eggs, beaten

3 Tbsp mayonnaise

3 Tbsp minced fresh chives

1½ Tbsp minced capers

1 Tbsp minced fresh dill

½ tsp Diamond Crystal kosher salt

8 oz [225 g] skinless cod fillets, or similar fresh
white-fleshed fish, cut into 1 in [2.5 cm] cubes

Five 1 in [2.5 cm] thick slices challah (page 125)
or white sandwich bread, crusts removed

2 cups [250 g] white sesame seeds

1 cup [240 g] vegetable oil or Schmaltz
(page 56) for frying

Dill pickle coins, Chinese hot mustard, and
lemon wedges for serving (optional)

*Our kosher take on Chinese shrimp toast,
a dim sum staple.*

Line a plate or a cooling rack with paper towels.

Place the fish in a medium bowl. Use your hands to gently flake the fish into small chunks. Add the eggs, mayonnaise, chives, capers, dill, salt, and the cod pieces to the bowl, and use a rubber spatula to gently mix everything until combined. In small batches, transfer the mixture to a food processor, and pulse until homogenous. The mixture should be smooth, moist, and pasty (not crumbly), with a slight sheen. Be careful not to overprocess or overfill the food processor, which would overheat the mixture. Return the paste to the medium bowl.

Using the back of a soup spoon or a butter knife, spread the paste over a slice of challah, covering the entire piece of bread evenly to the edges with a ⅜ in [1 cm] thick layer of fish paste. Repeat with the remaining paste and bread.

Rest the toasts for about 10 minutes. This will help the paste stick to the bread.

Scatter the sesame seeds on the bottom of a shallow container or small baking sheet, and press the toasts into the seeds, fish-side down, making sure the seeds are spread out evenly on the fish paste.

Heat the oil or schmaltz in a large nonstick sauté pan over medium heat until it begins to bubble, but is not near the point of smoking or browning. Place one or two toasts, seeded-side down, in the pan and cook until golden and toasty, about 3 to 4 minutes. Make sure to watch the heat, so the seeds don't get too brown. If they do, take the pan off the heat and let it cool down for a minute. Flip the bread to cook the bottoms until golden brown, 3 to 4 minutes more. Drain on the paper towels. Repeat with the remaining toasts.

Cut each slice of bread into four triangles and serve with pickles, mustard, and lemon wedges, as desired.

Everything Spice Crunchy Chili Oil

Makes 2 cups [480 ml]

½ cup [110 g] Everything Spice (recipe follows)

¼ cup [40 g] chili flakes

One 1½ in [4 cm] knob ginger, peeled and cut into ⅛ in [4 mm] thick coins

1 cup [240 ml] vegetable oil

1 Tbsp soy sauce

2 tsp sugar

Heat a small heavy-bottomed saucepan over medium-high heat. Add the Everything Spice and chili flakes and toast until very fragrant, stirring constantly to prevent burning and sticking, 4 to 5 minutes. Add the ginger and vegetable oil and stir with a wooden spoon to combine. Immediately remove from the heat. Let the mixture sit for 5 minutes to perfume the oil. Gently whisk in the soy sauce and sugar, and cool completely. Transfer to a glass jar with a tight-fitting lid and store in the refrigerator for up to 3 months.

Consider this sticky, textured sauce our Ashkenazi version of sririacha. It's got a slight kick (not too spicy), a hint of sweet, and a splash of salty soy, which adds a punch of umami. Drizzle it over avocado toast, a slice of pizza, or peak summer tomatoes, with a splash of good vinegar. We use standard pizza joint–style red chili flakes, but Korean chili flakes add a nice zip, too.

Everything Spice

2 Tbsp dehydrated chopped onion

1 Tbsp dehydrated minced garlic

2 Tbsp hulled white sesame seeds

1 Tbsp poppy seeds

1½ tsp whole caraway seeds

¾ tsp coarse or flaked sea salt

Heat a dry skillet or pan over medium heat. Do not use a nonstick surface. When the skillet is hot, add the onion, garlic, sesame seeds, poppy seeds, and caraway seeds. Toast until fragrant, about 3 minutes, shaking the skillet or stirring with a wooden spoon to avoid burning. Remove the skillet from the heat and let cool completely in the skillet. In a small bowl, toss the mixture with the salt to combine. Store in a jar with a tight-fitting lid in a cool, dark place for up to 3 months. Makes just under 1 cup [220 g].

Chinese Chicken Salad

Serves 2 (as a main dish)

Vegetable oil for frying

6 to 8 small wonton wrappers, sliced ⅛ in [4 mm] thick

Diamond Crystal kosher salt

8 cups [800 g] sliced Napa cabbage (1/16 in [2 mm] thick)

1 cup [100 g] sliced red cabbage (1/16 in [2 mm] thick)

1 cup [30 g] roughly chopped frisée or chicory

½ cup [25 g] shredded carrots

¼ cup [35 g] thinly sliced red onion

¼ cup [25 g] thinly sliced radishes

½ cup [65 g] cold shredded cooked chicken (page 55)

1 navel orange, cut into segments, peeled, and seeded

1 Tbsp pickled sushi ginger

⅓ cup [80 ml] Sweet Sesame Dressing (recipe follows)

8 to 10 sprigs cilantro and a generous pinch of toasted sesame seeds for garnish

This is a Wise Sons' staple, and an ode to our Southern California roots. If you have a mandoline, use it to slice the red onion and radishes.

In a large bowl, toss together the Napa cabbage, red cabbage, frisée, carrot, onion, and half the radishes until well combined. Add the chicken, half the orange segments, and half the ginger, and toss again. Add the dressing to the salad and toss well to combine. Taste to adjust the salt and amount of dressing. Transfer to a large shallow bowl or platter and garnish with the remaining radishes, oranges, and ginger, the cilantro, sesame seeds, and wontons. Serve immediately.

Line a rimmed baking sheet with paper towels. Heat 2 in [5 cm] of oil in a small saucepan over medium heat until bubbling. Slowly drop the sliced wonton wrappers into the hot oil, gently separating the strips with a fork if needed. Cook until golden brown, 1 to 2 minutes, and drain on the prepared baking sheet. Season lightly with salt and set aside.

Sweet Sesame Dressing

2 Tbsp mayonnaise

1½ Tbsp toasted sesame oil

1 Tbsp white wine vinegar

1 Tbsp low-sodium soy sauce

1 Tbsp sugar

1 tsp toasted sesame seeds

In a small bowl, whisk together the mayonnaise, sesame oil, vinegar, soy sauce, sugar, and sesame seeds and set aside. (The dressing can be stored in a tightly sealed container in the refrigerator for up to 2 weeks.) Makes 6 Tbsp [90 ml].

Ode to the Unofficial JCCs

Maybe it was because Jews weren't exactly embraced by the stuffy country clubs; or because everything else was closed on Sundays, per Puritan tradition; or because by the end of the weekend, no one wanted to cook, and Caviar and Uber Eats had yet to be invented. But for decades, in suburbs around the country, one night a week, Chinese American restaurants became de facto Jewish community centers, where Jewish families would organically commune at otherwise unremarkable establishments to see and be seen over pupu platters, spare ribs, beef and broccoli, and those cute little baby corns.

Sunday Night Chinese isn't as well known as its Christmas Day counterpart, of course. And yet the tradition quietly lives on in Jewish life. Although these days, instead of going out, it's become more of a gather-round-the-kitchen-table, takeout situation (see page 88). We might even order Thai or Burmese or Vietnamese, but—for whatever reason—our Sunday Asian cuisine cravings continue. According to Grubhub, Sunday is, indeed, still the most popular day of the week for Chinese delivery.

Is this a one-way relationship?

Why don't Chinese people gorge on Jewish food like Jews do on Chinese food?

"It's very obvious," says Ed Schoenfeld, a Jewish restaurateur and scholar of Chinese food in New York. "Chinese food is better."

Jennifer 8. Lee, author of *The Fortune Cookie Chronicles* (2008) and producer of the documentary film *The Search for General Tso*, agrees with Schoenfeld: "Chinese food is better." Chinese people like eating Chinese food so much, she says, that "they don't really need to eat other cuisines. Even when they're traveling to Italy or France or America, they seek out Chinese restaurants." However, Asian urbanites have fully adopted the deli. "I mean, we're not eating gefilte fish all day—but neither are you." Good point. Bagels, she admits, are a different beast. "We've fully embraced the bagel." A few years ago, a Chinese woman went back to Beijing and started making them there.

"If you think about it, it's not all that obvious how to eat a bagel," says Lee. "At first, her employees sliced them up and stir-fried them."

Pastrami Fried Rice

Serves 1

Grab your trusty cast-iron skillet. Dice **3 or 4 slices of pastrami** or **corned beef** and sauté until crispy and golden brown. Remove from the pan and set aside. Turn the heat up as high as it goes. Blast the pan for 3 to 4 minutes, until it's smoking—you might set off the smoke alarm, but that means you're doing it right. Add **2 Tbsp of vegetable oil** (this is fried rice, after all), and dump in **about 2 cups [240 g] of cooked rice** (about a medium-size Chinese restaurant takeout container is what you're going for). Break up the rice and toss it around in the oil for a few minutes with a small metal spatula. Do your best Benihana impression. Squeeze in a **takeout packet's worth (2 tsp) of soy sauce** and maybe a **pinch of salt**, and mix it all up until uniformly light brown in color. Toss it around some more. Shake the pan. Clean up the rice you inevitably tossed right out of the pan. Throw in **some thinly sliced scallions**, both the white and green parts, and shake, shake, shake. Make a small well in the middle of the pan and add **an egg**. Scramble it, and then mix it up with the rice. Return the pastrami to the pan, and add a small **squirt of sambal** or **sriracha**, if you're feisty. Guess what? Toss it some more! For a professional look, pack it tightly into a bowl and invert it onto a plate so you have a Chinese restaurant–like mound of fried rice. Add some crispy things for garnish: **french-fried onion rings**, **toasted sesame seeds**, **peanuts**—whatever you've got. (For more pastrami recipes, see page 26.)

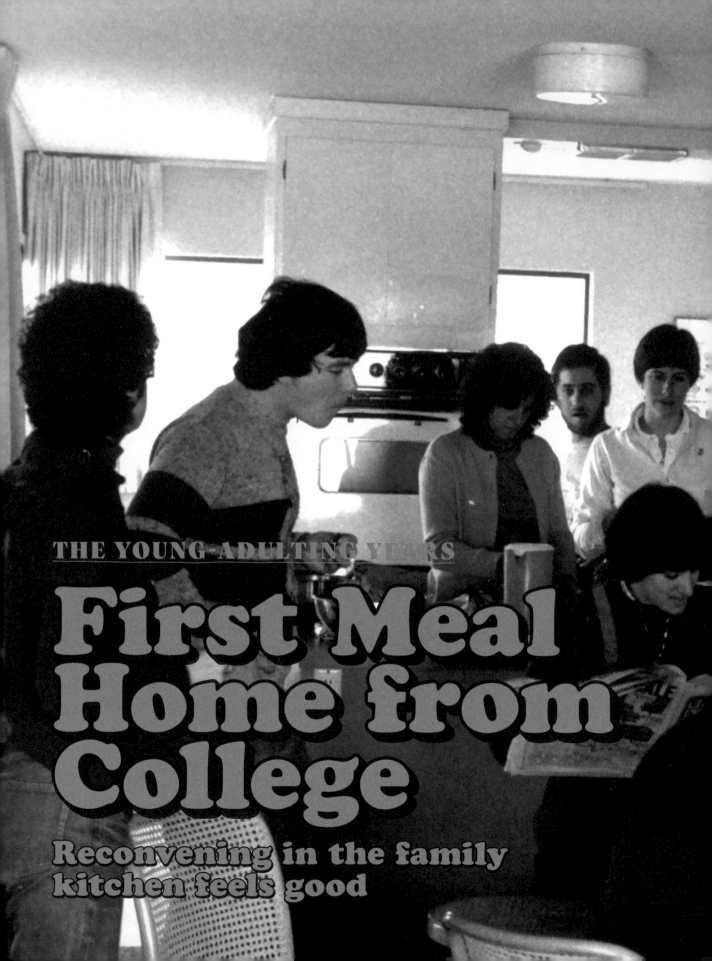

First Meal Home from College

Reconvening in the family kitchen feels good

"Feed Me, Mom"

*Yes, of course, there are a handful of Jewish mothers who don't cook. "I'm a shiksa who nannied for a kosher Jewish family in Beverly Hills. The stay-at-home mom didn't cook, but the Guatemalan housekeeper did. I learned about keeping separate 'leche' and 'carne' plates from a three-year-old in broken Spanglish."

—Kathryn, from Texas

There are, in general, two types of Jewish mothers: those who cook and are good at it, and those who cook and aren't good at it.* And no matter which kind of mother we have, we grow up eating her food and loving it.

Each dish takes on its own kind of iconic status within the family. We come to know these dishes as well as we know the contours of our childhood kitchens. The silverware is in the drawer below the toaster, the butter is in the refrigerator, and the meat loaf is a gray-hued hunk, soft diced onions buried within and a sweet, warm coat of Heinz ketchup on top. The lasagna is a Pyrex full of Barilla noodles with curled, burnt edges and a filling made with a jar of sugary Ragú and a scattering of crispy beef crumbles.

And the sweet-and-sour meatballs—oh, the sweet-and-sour meatballs!—were, and remain, a favorite. An unrefined recipe found in old spiral-bound sisterhood cookbooks, in recipe collections like June Roth's *How to Cook Like a Jewish Mother* (1993), and on tattered, yellowed, hand-scrawled recipe cards around the country. Typically, the dish consists of beef, molded into "bawls" (as Grandma Frances would say), with cabbage, maybe, and was it Welch's grape jelly? Or crushed gingersnaps? Or a can of Ocean Spray cranberry sauce and Lipton onion soup mix and Heinz ketchup and Dole crushed pineapple. (Shout-out to Aunt Shelley of Dallas!) Whatever it was, it was passed down from grandmother to mother to daughter until it became the foodstuff of Jewish family lore.

Whether or not it's actually any good is not the point. The point is: Every Jewish mother mourns the day her child leaves her dinner table.

"It was devastating," says Evan's mom, Linda. "It still is." She used to cook every night for her sons: steak fajitas, barbecue chicken, meatballs. Except her meatballs were a little more sophisticated: currants and shallots, maybe some pine nuts. "Grape jelly? Yuck," she says. "Never."

Whatever your mother, Jewish or otherwise, cooked for you as a kid, she will miss cooking it for you when you go off to college (and you will go off to college, she will make sure of it)—and she will cook it for you when you come home.

And after a semester of dining hall fare and late-night drunken pizza, you will like it as much as you used to. One day, you might be moved to make it yourself. And maybe you'll even make it better.

Sweet & Sour Meatballs

Makes 25 to 30 meatballs

MEATBALLS

1 lb [455 g] 80/20 ground beef
(80 percent lean beef and 20 percent fat)

1 large egg, lightly beaten

½ cup [80 g] grated yellow onion,
with liquid (about ½ a medium onion)

1½ tsp Diamond Crystal kosher salt

¼ tsp freshly ground black pepper

½ cup [70 g] fine dry bread crumbs

1 Tbsp vegetable oil

SAUCE

One 12 oz [360 ml] can pineapple juice

3 Tbsp soy sauce

2 Tbsp apple cider vinegar

½ tsp Worcestershire sauce

¼ cup [50 g] golden brown sugar

2 Tbsp tomato paste

2 Tbsp cornstarch

¼ cup [60 ml] hot water

To make the meatballs, in a large mixing bowl, combine the ground beef, egg, onion, salt, and pepper. Using clean hands, mix until well blended. Slowly add the bread crumbs, a little at a time, working them into the meat mixture until evenly combined. Form into small balls by rolling 1½ Tbsp of meat between your hands. Set aside the meatballs on a large plate or baking sheet.

I'm not really sure when this dish became "Jewish," but it was certainly a staple of my grandmother's repertoire, and probably yours. Most of the iterations call for dumping either Welch's grape jelly or Heinz chili sauce (or both) into the Crock-Pot. It's sort of Chinese, sort of Swedish, sort of sweet-and-sour cabbage from the old country, and very American. Skip the slow cooker and sear the meatballs first. My safta added sliced pineapples or green bell peppers for garnish.

Heat the oil in large cast-iron skillet or other heavy-bottomed pan over medium-high heat. Working in batches, sear the meatballs, undisturbed, for 2 to 3 minutes until well browned, and turn with a wooden spoon and sear for 2 minutes more. Remove the meatballs from the pan using a slotted spoon and set aside.

To make the sauce, in a medium Dutch oven or large saucepan over medium heat, combine the pineapple juice, soy sauce, vinegar, and Worcestershire sauce. Whisk lightly to combine and heat until the liquid simmers lightly, 4 to 5 minutes. Add the brown sugar and the tomato paste, whisking well until smooth. Turn the heat to medium-low.

In a small bowl, whisk together the cornstarch and hot water until smooth to create a slurry. Slowly add the slurry to the hot sauce mixture, whisking constantly to create a smooth sauce. Return the heat to medium and carefully add the seared meatballs to the pan, stirring to coat. Cook for 8 to 10 minutes, until the sauce is glossy and coats the back of a spoon and the meatballs are cooked through. Serve immediately with toothpicks. These can be made in advance and stored in an airtight container in the refrigerator for up to 3 days. Reheat the meatballs in the sauce over medium-low heat for 10 to 12 minutes.

Ode to Our Parents' Pantry*

Caffeine-free Diet Coke
(Mom's second secret ingredient in
brisket, and also favorite beverage)

**Frozen concentrated
orange juice**
("fresher" than the carton)

Welch's grape jelly
(a must in sweet-and-sour
meatballs, and spread on
toast on sick days)

Manischewitz wine
(always there, gathering dust)

Lipton's French onion soup mix
(also for brisket)

Prunes (Grandma's morning
laxative, and morning gin-soaked
treat [see page 113])

Sara Lee pound cake
(the freezer had more aluminum
foil pans of Sara Lee than ice cubes)

We still kind of love all of this stuff, by the way . . .

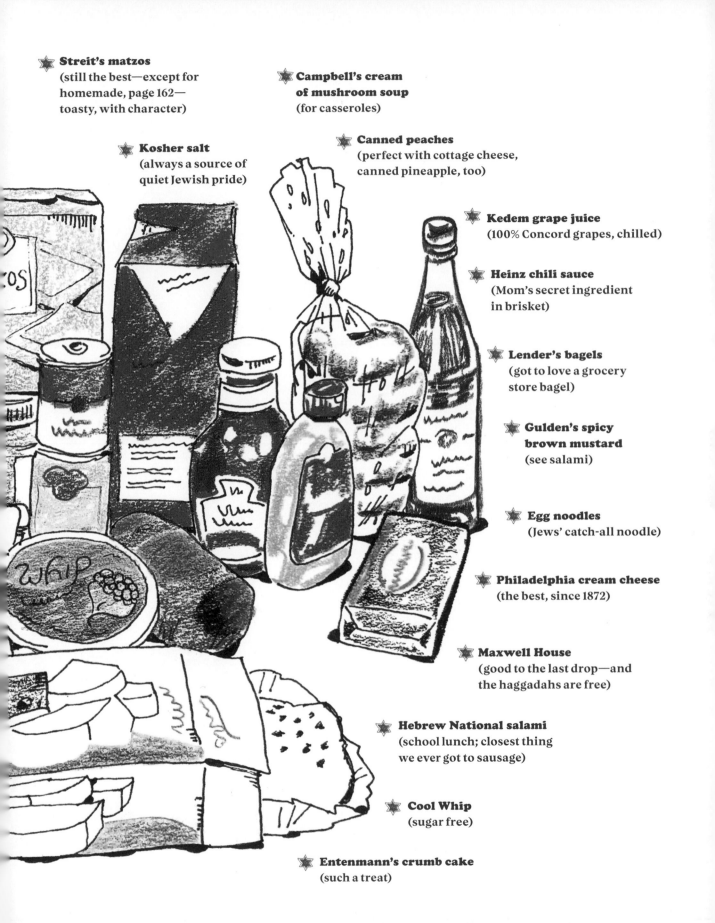

⭐ **Streit's matzos**
(still the best—except for homemade, page 162—toasty, with character)

⭐ **Campbell's cream of mushroom soup**
(for casseroles)

⭐ **Kosher salt**
(always a source of quiet Jewish pride)

⭐ **Canned peaches**
(perfect with cottage cheese, canned pineapple, too)

⭐ **Kedem grape juice**
(100% Concord grapes, chilled)

⭐ **Heinz chili sauce**
(Mom's secret ingredient in brisket)

⭐ **Lender's bagels**
(got to love a grocery store bagel)

⭐ **Gulden's spicy brown mustard**
(see salami)

⭐ **Egg noodles**
(Jews' catch-all noodle)

⭐ **Philadelphia cream cheese**
(the best, since 1872)

⭐ **Maxwell House**
(good to the last drop—and the haggadahs are free)

⭐ **Hebrew National salami**
(school lunch; closest thing we ever got to sausage)

⭐ **Cool Whip**
(sugar free)

⭐ **Entenmann's crumb cake**
(such a treat)

J Dating

Oh, the pressure

"Are You Meeting New People? (I Hope They're the Right Kind.)"
—Evan's safta

It's a sentiment all too often expressed by Jewish grandmothers. By all grandmothers, really. Indian grandmothers. Greek grandmothers. Korean grandmothers. Often mothers, and fathers, too—they'd just never come out and say it. Pretty much every first- or second- or third-generation immigrant parent would prefer their precious offspring breed with their own. (I mean, my mom was as susceptible as I was to my old WASPy ex-boyfriend's Aussie charm and accent, but she was absolutely over the moon when I brought home a fellow Ashkenazi who hailed from the exotic land of Upstate New York.)

This pressure "to date our kind" is something we can't help but feel, at some point in our lives, on some level. It's a desire that ebbs and flows, like love itself. As Molly Tolsky, editor of *Hey Alma*, an online magazine "for millennial women with chutzpah," wrote: "It's definitely starting to become 'hotter' to me when someone is a Jew. Before, I was much more attracted to people from different backgrounds . . . who had different experiences than me. But now if a dude makes a joke about gefilte fish, I'm like, 'Marry me.'"

Judging by the number of Jewish dating sites alone, one might deduce that Jews feel this pressure the most. There's JDate (dated) and JMatch (free JDate) and JSwipe (Jewish Tinder), and JCrush (tagline: "Make your bubbe happy! Connect with Jewish singles and find your beshert."). SawYouAtSinai, almost twenty years old, claims an impressive 3,200 marriages among its 40,000 mostly Orthodox members. There are also "youth" groups and live events with not-so-blatant find-love undertones, like "Late Shabbats" and "Matzo Balls" and adult sleep-together (oops, I mean sleepaway) camps like Trybal Gatherings.

Lately, though, Jews seem to be getting jaded, not about the importance of dating other Jews (that will always be a debate), but about how to go about meeting them. Tired of swiping and scrolling, some are reverting back to the analog ways of the old days, of the old world, of the old-fashioned matchmaker, or shadchan.

Not long ago, JDate launched a clever ad campaign to help revive its almost quarter-century-old site. The fresh face of its brand? A wizened ninety-year-old woman—a coding whiz wearing a sweat suit. "Mensch-Seeking Machine," read the billboards, along with the company's new tagline: "Powered by Yentas." Yentas with an algorithm.

An algorithm that arguably can't compare to the efforts of real-life yentas, as evidenced by the 150 singles who once filled out online questionnaires so they could be set up on dates by the Yentas of Temple Emanu-El, in San Francisco.

No matter how you meet your maybe-match, though, you're most likely going to meet over a meal. Even if that meal is only a martini. But as everyone knows, a successful first date is followed by dinner. And if that goes well it, uh, morphs into breakfast. And then another dinner. And then brunch. And then a midweek "Hey, honey, want to grab lunch?" Then meal-kit cooking. Or better: real cooking. Then eating together all the time, plotting every supper like you might, eventually, your retirement. Until, maybe one day, you break up and you're not.

"We hired a yenta, and out of ten set-ups, she had three marriages! Three marriages! That's better than any algorithm."
—Rabbi Ryan Bauer

Manny's Morning After Matzoquiles

Serves 2

2 sheets matzo, broken into large pieces

4 large eggs, beaten

2 tsp vegetable oil

¼ tsp Diamond Crystal kosher salt

½ cup [120 ml] Tomatillo Sauce (recipe follows)

Fresh cilantro leaves, sour cream, thinly sliced white onion, sliced radishes, crumbled cotija cheese, and sliced avocado (in any combination) for serving

In a medium bowl, combine the matzo pieces and eggs and set aside for 5 minutes to soak. Heat the oil in a large nonstick skillet over medium-high heat until sizzling. Add the matzo mixture to the pan and season with the salt. Cook for 2 minutes for soft eggs, stirring often to scramble the eggs, but folding the ingredients carefully so as not to turn the matzo into mush.

Add the tomatillo sauce and cook until hot, another 30 seconds. Serve immediately in a shallow bowl, with the toppings of your choice alongside.

Mazto brei was as common in my house as pancakes were at all my friends'. It's a messy scramble of broken-up matzo and eggs, and every family has their way of making it. Some like it sweet, some like it savory. At Wise Sons, we like it spicy. Our chef Manny and our kitchen crew came up with this version one Passover, and it's been a favorite ever since. The sauce freezes extremely well, so feel free to double or triple it—it's great for braising chicken, too.

Tomatillo Sauce

1½ lb [680 g] tomatillos, husked

2 jalapeño chiles, stemmed

1 medium yellow onion, peeled and quartered

2 garlic cloves, peeled and trimmed

1 Tbsp olive oil

½ tsp Diamond Crystal kosher salt

Preheat the oven to 450°F [230°C]. In a large bowl, toss the tomatillos, jalapeños, onion, garlic, oil, and salt until well coated. Transfer the mixture to a large baking sheet. Bake for 12 to 15 minutes, until fragrant and the tomatillos are soft, but not quite bursting. Remove from the oven and set aside to cool slightly, 10 to 15 minutes.

Transfer the tomatillo mixture to a blender or food processor, and purée until smooth. Let cool. If not using right away, store in an airtight container in the refrigerator for up to 1 week. This sauce freezes well, for up to 3 months. Makes about 2½ cups [590 ml].

Real-Life Food Stories from the Frontlines of Dating While Jewish

- "I would've loved to meet someone Jewish. But then I met Leah. She was not Jewish. Yeah, I know, even though her name's Leah. But when she told me her favorite sandwich is a pastrami Reuben, I knew we could make it work."

- "I'm a food lover who grew up with a mother who couldn't cook for shit. I ended up marrying an Italian woman. That wasn't by accident. I thought: Wouldn't God want us to be happy? Her lasagna was so good, my mom forgave me."

- "I once dated a guy who told me that he'd eat his food in pill form if he could. That was more or less the end of that."

- "So, I love charoset. I used to have a crush on one of my brother's friends, the kind of crush where I didn't want to date him now, I just thought we should get married later. Until he came to Passover Seder. He made the charoset— and it was awful. Like, really bad. I started spiraling into extreme forward thinking. (Like, now I'm going to have to eat this charoset for the rest of my life. I wanted our future kids to love charoset, too, and now they'll hate charoset.) But then I realized: Wait! I don't have to marry this guy! I don't even like him that much. I like charoset more."

- "It was a requirement that any man I seriously dated love Russ & Daughters. I used to use it as a litmus test."

- "I'm kosher. My girlfriend is more or less, too—except for pulled pork; she really loves pulled pork. Early in our relationship, we were out to lunch and she ordered a pulled-pork sandwich. She ate it and then went to kiss me, and I was like, 'No, not for another thirty minutes!' She didn't kiss me for a few days after that."

- "Once I went on a date with someone who kept kosher, and I was like, 'Sorry, this just isn't going to work.' He kept emailing me, saying, 'We can figure it out!' and I kept replying, 'Nope. I'm not going to live in a kosher house.' Now my boyfriend is a guy named Blair (not a Jew, obviously)."

- "My husband used to date a shiksa, a WASPy, pearl-wearing woman. Until one romantic weekend away in Napa, he had a revelation when they were out to dinner, eating steak, and she ordered a glass of milk with their bottle of Cab. He was like, 'That's it. Too much.' He broke up with her. And then met me."

- "I started dating again at eighty-six, after my wife of sixty-one years passed away. The women love that I can drive to a restaurant at night. Very desirable skill here in Palm Beach, Florida. The only problem is figuring out what restaurant we can actually get into. The Grill is very good, but it's always mobbed. It's 5:30 or 9:30! I'm no early bird—only imbeciles dine at 5:30. And 9:30 is too late—especially when all the women want sex. But after my prostate treatment, I haven't really been, uh, up for it."

Bagel Texting (Bexting?)

"My Bumble profile says 'full of optimism, joy, and strong opinions on the proper way to eat a bagel.' (Maybe I should be using the Coffee-Meets-Bagel app?) Anyway, I get so many notes from guys about bagels. A few of my favorites:

'What is the proper way to eat a bagel? I'm a Jew by birth so I'm ashamed I don't know the answer.' —Maury

'Well, now I'm craving a bagel.' —Matt

'Tell me. I fear I've been doing it wrong this whole time.' —Sanjay

'Because you care: I always eat my bagel open-faced. Otherwise it feels like the whole ratio of bagel to toppings is off. Lox is my favorite topping, but if it's served as a sandwich, it's so hard to separate the halves and evenly distribute the capers and onions.' —Paul

I was totally into Paul. Until he started sending me bagel pics. It was like sexting, but with photos of bagel orders gone wrong. Every morning, I got a new bagel text.

But then we never went out! Not even for bagels."

—Jourdan, from San Francisco

Hi, Jourdan, I like your profile. I like bagels, too. Tell me: What IS the proper way to eat a bagel?

Hi, Matt! The absolute best way to eat a bagel is open-faced with cream cheese and toppings on both halves. There is a NY bagel sandwich exemption if you're eating it on the go, but cream cheese must be applied to both halves, and the toppings, too—which allows you to eat it open-faced when you arrive at your destination. Nothing enrages me quite like a poorly made bagel sandwich where there's a lump of cream cheese on one half and then tomato slices which have made the other side soggy and sad.

I think I just swooned. How do you feel about chives in your cream cheese? I think they add a nice texture + flavor.

I hate chives in my cream cheese. Unless they're fresh. To be clear, most chive cream cheese is actually scallion cream cheese. But chives are obviously the superior choice.

Well, now I'm craving a bagel, with real chive cream cheese, Nova, capers, tomato—and YOU. Any chance you're free tonight?

I don't usually eat bagels at night. But . . . if it's toasted, and topped with tuna, sure.

On Drinks & Drinking

> "A good way to tell the gentiles from the Jews is to watch them leave the theater. Because every gentile says the same thing: `Have a drink?` `Have a drink?' And every Jew will be saying the same thing, too: `Did you eat yet?'"
>
> —Jackie Mason in *The World According to Me!*, a Tony Award–winning, one-man show, which opened on Broadway in 1986

My mom went through a fleeting Cosmopolitan phase, meaning she had one once, at my sister's wedding. And then, I think, another four years later at mine? Otherwise, my mother's excuse, common among her Jewish middle- and upper-middle-class cohort, never seems to hold much water: "I just don't like the taste," she always says. Evan's mom says it makes her feel "tired and bloated." When I asked a Barbara Streisand–Carole King look-alike I know, from Venice Beach, she mulled it over for a moment and then said: "I don't know why. Maybe it's because we liked to smoke pot more?"

There's the old Catskills-era joke, of course, which only confirmed the Ashkenazi stereotype. ("Why don't Jewish mothers drink?" "Alcohol interferes with their suffering." Ha, ha.) But where did this joke come from? Why don't our grandmothers and mothers drink booze like, um, their daughters do?

"Among Eastern European immigrants and their descendants, there was a feeling of otherness, of vulnerability," says Marni Davis, associate professor at Georgia State University and author of *Jews and Booze* (2014). "As Kant said, 'Intoxication . . . deprives one of cautiousness.' And so as a marginalized, vulnerable population, Jews viewed drunkenness as dangerous. Goyish. Our grandparents and parents may not have found the effects of alcohol pleasurable, but as Jews assimilated into diverse public schools and mainstream universities, that became less and less true"— for Jewish women, especially. "Although I haven't seen any studies done at Sigma Delta Tau," she jokes.

Jewish men, however. They drank. Even if the prevailing belief back in nineteenth-century Poland was otherwise.

"Jews are always sober," a Polish noble and social reformer once put it. Or as Sarah Lawrence professor Glenn Dynner titled his 2014 paper on Jewish drinking practices and the sobriety stereotype in Eastern Europe: "A Jewish Drunk Is Hard to Find." Not true, at least among the Hasidic and Orthodox sects of that time, which were the focus of his paper.

Meanwhile, when it came to Jewish fathers of a certain generation, their Eastern European heritage was quite clear. My dad did the classic come-home-from-work-loosen-the-tie-pour-a-glass-of-Absolut-on-the-rocks thing. Adding his signature Danny Levin nightly twist: a few cubes of cut-up cantaloupe or blueberries from the refrigerator. He was way ahead of the fruit-infused booze trend. As was Evan's Nana . . .

The Goldie

Makes 1 drink

Every morning my Nana Goldie ate a prune soaked in gin. To keep her regular, she said. No guarantee boozy prunes will keep you kicking until ninety-seven, like Goldie, but I'm not saying they won't, either. Enjoy as a morning treat like my grandmother, or try our Goldie cocktail at night.

In a 1 qt [960 ml] glass jar with a tight-fitting lid, mix **1 cup [240 mL] of gin**, **8 oz [225 g] of pitted prunes**, and the **grated zest of 1 lemon**. Cover and store in the refrigerator for at least 2 weeks and up to 2 months. When you're ready to make the cocktail, combine **equal parts prune-infused gin**, **Campari**, and **sweet vermouth** over **large cubes of ice** in a rocks glass.

Garnish with a **strip of orange peel** and a **marinated prune**. Makes 1 drink, and about 3 cups [720 ml] prunes in gin.

Bloody Moishe

Makes 1 drink

Wise Sons was born in San Francisco's Mission District, the historic Latino center of the city. This is our ode to the famous hangover-curing hair of the dog, the michelada.

Grab a 1 pt [480 ml] glass and fill it with about ¼ **cup [60 ml] tomato juice** (or Clamato—treyf!). Add **1 Tbsp of prepared hot horseradish**, **1 tsp of Worcestershire sauce**, a **squeeze of lemon or lime**, **1 pinch of black pepper**, and **1 pinch of salt**. We like to add a **splash of Tapatío hot sauce** and, if you've got it, **1 tsp of Basic Brine** (page 216). Mix well. Add a few **ice cubes** and pour in a **12 oz [360 ml] beer**. **Pickle spears** or **lemon wedges** make it festive.

You could also make the base by the batch—just be sure to keep it in the refrigerator, sealed tightly. It should keep for 2 or 3 days.

Ode to the Old Bar

Whiskey

My Grandpa Sam kept his fledgling liquor collection in a simple Formica hutch in the living room, nothing fancy, but it did the job. He'd take his nightly swig from the bottle of Seagram's VO, wipe his chin, and sit down to dinner.

Today
Trendy Japanese whisky with, say, Lillet Blanc and amaretto

Caffeine-Free Diet Coke

Evan's grandparents swore by it. My mother guzzled it, for decades. "I'm off it now," she said. "But I loved the bubbles, and it always settled my tummy after a big meal. Seltzer just doesn't do the same," Mom explained. "Growing up we weren't allowed to have milk with dinner. You know, the *milchig* (dairy) and *fleishig* (meat) divide. Water wasn't a thing then, and neither was caffeine-free or diet cola. So, I always had Pepsi with meat meals." But then, caffeine-free Coke came along, and Pepsi, as everyone knows, became second fiddle.

Today
Mixologist-made craft soda

Peach Schnapps

"We always had it in the house, but no one ever drank it," says Evan. "It lived in our bar, never touched. Until my brother and I got to high school, and started stealing swigs."

Today
Amaro

Seltzer

Jewish Champagne, delivered. Grandpa Sam, sitting in his apartment in Fort Lee, New Jersey, at the head of his plastic-wrapped dining room table, the Hudson River behind him, spritzing fizzy water from the cloudy-blue glass bottle into his glass, was as much an event as any cork popped on the old-monied Upper East Side.

Today
LaCroix by the case

Dr. Brown's Cel-Ray Soda

Created in 1869 by a mysterious man, or marketing ploy, named Dr. Brown. A celery tonic with the promise of settling stomachs, it was initially sold door to door by Jewish salesmen, and later (through the 1980s), exclusively to delis, along with other cult favorites—black cherry soda and cream soda. Still a perfect pairing with pastrami.

Today
Turmeric tonic

White Zinfandel

White Zin. Low alcohol, lots of sugar. Insufficiently fermented and overly sweet, it was the wine for people who didn't like wine (i.e., Jewish women of a certain generation). And from the day Napa Valley's Sutter Home released it in 1975, it was a serious hit that lasted into the early '90s.

Today
Rosé. All day.

Crown Royal

Never saw Grandpa Sam, or my parents, or anyone actually drink the stuff. But one velvet purple bag hung on the bathroom doorknob by its braided, golden-yellow chain, full of Mom's dirty stockings waiting to be washed out. Another lived inside the Scrabble box, holding the clanky tiles. Still does.

Today
Cocktails in chic cans

Shabbat

Everyone's doing it

HA[...]
MINNIE
META
194

Friday Night Lighting

I got a text the other day: "You guys want to come over for Shabbat dinner on Friday?" Shabbat dinner on Friday. It was a subtle thing, a nuance only a true Jew would notice, but still, a dead giveaway—as Shabbat dinner could *only* be on Friday.

No matter. My non-Jewish friends are so into Shabbat, they've made it a verb. As in: "Let's Shabbat." Or, "We're Shabbat-ing." (Catchy, right?)

And they're not alone. Cooking a Friday feast with family and friends and powering down after a long workweek needs no religious affiliation, really. And yet: Our ancient tradition is trending.

Everyone could just call it a dinner party. Or "Netflix and Chill." Or takeout Thai. Except they're not. They're calling it Shabbat because it connotes what they're ultimately craving: offline connection, community, a nourishing end-of-week antidote to an otherwise tumultuous world. Oh, and of course, roast chicken.

Not long ago, a New Yorker named Aliza Kline launched a new social-dining platform devoted to Shabbat dinners called OneTable (tagline: "How do you Friday?"), infusing new life into an age-old ritual. They offer hosts food money, Shabbat coaching, even a challah hotline. The goal is to make Shabbat easy, accessible, and appealing. "It's going gangbusters," says Kline. On any given Friday night, there are hundreds of OneTable suppers happening in postcollege apartments in cities around the country. Imagine, some 100,000 (and counting) twentysomethings a year, of all faiths, sitting down together for Shabbat dinner. Without their parents. That's something.

Natalie Portman does it. "Shabbat is the one day we can stop time," she once wrote, paraphrasing twentieth-century philosopher-psychologist Erich Fromm.

Meanwhile, there's a WASPy middle-aged mother of three who Shabbats more religiously than any Jew I know. Not because her husband is a MOT, but because she likes the idea that Friday nights are for family, for coming together around

the kitchen table, for taking a collective pause, no matter what the weekend throws their way.

Ashton Kutcher, husband of Russian-born Jew Mila Kunis, does it. He once posted a photo of two candles aglow, with an unwitting comment: "SS." No, not the Schutzstaffel, who were Nazi soldiers. He meant it as a shorthand for Shabbat Shalom, because, you know, he's busy. It got 20,000 Likes within the hour. Supermodel and Jewish convert Karlie Kloss does it. "[Shabbat] helps me reconnect to the actual world," she told *British Vogue*. And pop star Katy Perry, raised an evangelical Christian, wants to do it. "I wish there was a thing like Shabbat for the whole world," she has said.

Well, Katy Perry, now it seems there is.

Jewish Chicken

Serves 3 to 4

1 Tbsp plus 2 tsp Diamond Crystal kosher salt

1 Tbsp sweet paprika

1 tsp freshly ground black pepper,
plus more for seasoning

1 tsp onion powder

1 tsp garlic powder

3 Tbsp fresh lemon juice, lemon reserved

One 4 lb [1.8 kg] whole chicken, giblets removed

2 medium russet potatoes, peeled and
cut into 1 in [2.5 cm] cubes

2 large carrots, peeled, halved lengthwise,
and cut into 1 in [2.5 cm] lengths

½ medium yellow onion, cut into small wedges

3 Tbsp vegetable oil

Shabbat dinner is synonymous with roast chicken. Once you realize how effortless it is to make it—yes, even on a Friday night after work—you'll want to do it every week. The key is seasoning a dry chicken ahead of time, and letting it rest in the refrigerator, uncovered. Look for an "air-chilled" chicken at the grocery store, which just means it doesn't have the added water content of a conventional bird and will roast better. The crispy paprika-and-schmaltz-bathed potatoes bring me right back to Shabbat dinner at Camp Alonim. When testing this recipe, a friend told me it was "too good to be Jewish roast chicken," which is sad. Just because Jewish chicken isn't spit roasted or southern fried or barbecued doesn't make it bland. Especially not this Jewish chicken.

In a small bowl, whisk together 1 Tbsp plus 1 tsp of the salt, the paprika, pepper, onion powder, and garlic powder until well combined. Add the lemon juice and stir until well mixed. Set aside.

Over an empty sink, use paper towels to pat the chicken dry thoroughly inside and out. This will take a few minutes, but the chicken will be better because of it. Place the chicken in a large bowl or on a large rimmed baking sheet. Using your hand, slather all the lemon-spice mixture over the entire bird, getting into all of the crevices and inside the cavity. This might seem like a lot of salt, but rest assured, it's not. Stick the juiced lemon inside the bird.

Place the spice-rubbed chicken, breast-side up, on a small baking sheet or rimmed plate.

Extra points if you have a rack to slip under the chicken, but it's not necessary. Pull the legs apart slightly so there is decent exposure to the air for maximum drying. Put the baking sheet on the bottom shelf of the refrigerator, uncovered—the circulation of the cool air will help dry and firm up the skin, while the lemon juice tenderizes the meat and the salt penetrates the thicker parts of the bird.

Let the bird rest in the refrigerator for at least 2 hours and up to 2 days.

Preheat the oven to 425°F [220°C].

In a large bowl, toss the potatoes, carrots, and onion with 1 Tbsp of the oil and the remaining 1 tsp of kosher salt. Set aside.

Heat the remaining 2 Tbsp of oil in a large cast-iron skillet over medium heat until shimmering. Gently place the chicken in the center, breast-side up. Scatter the potatoes, onion, and carrots around the bird, placing some of them underneath the legs and wings to prop them up. The pan will seem crowded.

continued

Roast in the center of the oven for 50 to 60 minutes, until the juices run clear when you pierce the center of a thigh with the tip of knife, or an instant-read thermometer registers 165°F [75°C]. Leave the oven on and, using oven mitts, carefully transfer the chicken to a large carving board or platter. Let rest for 10 to 15 minutes before carving.

Meanwhile, use a wooden spoon to toss the vegetables with all of juice in the pan. Return the skillet to the oven for 8 to 12 minutes, until the sugars have caramelized and the potatoes have a nice, evenly browned surface. Remove the pan from the oven and use a slotted spoon to scoop the vegetables onto a platter. Garnish with a few grinds of pepper.

Carve the chicken, and serve immediately. The chicken will keep, covered, in the refrigerator for up to 4 days, but the vegetables will be best enjoyed right away, as they will become a bit stale in the refrigerator.

✡ **You can get creative with the vegetables; Evan's wife Jessica's personal favorite is thinly sliced Japanese sweet potatoes, which get supercrisp from the schmaltz and the cast-iron skillet. Figure on using 1 tsp of salt per 1 lb [455 g] of chicken, plus 1 tsp more for the vegetables.**

Next Generation Health Salad

Serves 4

2 Tbsp apple cider vinegar

1 Tbsp sugar

1 tsp olive oil

2 generous handfuls sliced radicchio, chicory, treviso, endive, or a combination

4 cups [60 g] thinly sliced Lacinato kale

2 red radishes, thinly sliced, preferably on a mandoline

1 small carrot, peeled and shaved into ribbons with a vegetable peeler

1 small shallot, thinly sliced

Diamond Crystal kosher salt

Freshly ground black pepper

In a small bowl, whisk together the vinegar, sugar, and olive oil. Set aside.

Health salad is a classic Jewish deli side dish, something cabbagey I remember eating as a kid at the original 2nd Ave Deli in New York, where it came gratis to the table along with the pickles. There wasn't too much that was healthy about it; it was basically coleslaw made with a lot of sugar—but no mayonnaise. (Healthy!) We substitute kale and bitter lettuces for the cabbage, and skip the classic-but-questionable addition of green pepper, opting instead for thinly sliced radish. And still no mayonnaise. It is great for cutting rich foods, is easy to throw together, and holds up if it's dressed in advance—perfect for a family Shabbat meal prep.

Add the salad greens, kale, radishes, carrot, and shallot to a large salad serving bowl. Pour in the dressing and season with salt and the pepper. Use your hands to toss together, and then massage the dressing into the kale—you can't get the same effect with salad tongs or spoons. Let the tossed salad rest for at least 15 minutes or up to 1 hour before serving.

Wise Sons' Braided Challah

Makes 1 large six-strand loaf, or 2 smaller three-strand loaves

DOUGH

1 package (2¼ tsp) active dry yeast

½ cup [120 ml] warm water

3 cups [420 g] bread flour

¼ cup [60 ml] canola oil

3 Tbsp honey

2 large eggs, plus 3 egg yolks

2 Tbsp sugar

2½ tsp Diamond Crystal kosher salt

WASH AND TOPPING

1 large egg

1 Tbsp sesame seeds

1 Tbsp poppy seeds

Challah was the first baked good we made when we had the idea for Wise Sons. If you don't serve good challah, why bother? we thought. We tried quite a few recipes before landing on one that gained richness from extra egg yolks and a complex sweetness from a combination of honey and sugar. It's a versatile bread that's great for all sorts of uses. We offer a few options here, but we've been known to use it universally as a mother dough—from sufganiyot to Belgian-style waffles.

To make the dough, if you will be making it in a cold environment, preheat the oven to 175°F [80°C], and then turn it off. When the dough is ready for each rise, pop the covered bowl of dough in the warm, turned-off oven.

Combine the yeast and warm water in a small bowl and stir to dissolve the yeast. Set aside. In the bowl of a stand mixer fitted with the paddle attachment (or in a large bowl, using a handheld mixer), combine ½ cup [70 g] of the flour, the oil, honey, eggs, egg yolks, sugar, salt, and the dissolved yeast and water. Mix on low speed for about 45 seconds to combine. Stop to scrape down the bowl and make sure everything is incorporated. Don't worry if the flour is lumpy at this stage. With the mixer running at the lowest speed, gradually add the remaining 2½ cups [350 g] of flour and mix for another 30 seconds to combine well. Scrape the paddle and bowl, and replace the paddle with the dough hook. Knead the dough on medium-low speed for about 10 minutes, stopping midway through to scrape the sides and bottom of the bowl. When done, the dough should be smooth and elastic and pulling away from the sides of the bowl in one slightly tacky ball.

Alternatively you can make the dough by hand: Follow the preceding directions, mixing the ingredients with a wooden spoon. When you've stirred in the last of the flour, transfer the dough to a floured work surface and knead by hand for about 10 minutes, until smooth and elastic.

Scrape the dough into a large, lightly oiled bowl, turning to coat the dough with oil. Cover with a clean kitchen towel and let rise in a warm, draft-free place for 1 to 1½ hours, until puffy and almost double in size. Punch down and knead the dough a few times in the bowl. (At this point, you can freeze the dough to use later. Transfer to a lightly oiled 9 by 5 in [23 by 12 cm] loaf pan. Cover the pan tightly with plastic wrap and store in the freezer for up to 3 months. To defrost, remove the plastic wrap, cover the pan with a clean kitchen towel, and

continued

thaw completely at room temperature or in the refrigerator.)

Cover the dough with a kitchen towel and let rise a second time for about 1 hour, until doubled in size.

Line a standard 13 by 18 in [33 by 46 cm] half-sheet pan with parchment paper. After the second rise, punch down the dough and divide it into six equal pieces. Form each one into a log and place on the prepared baking pan. Cover loosely with a kitchen towel and let the dough rest for 10 minutes.

To braid a six-strand challah, with your hands, roll out each log of dough on a work surface, starting from the center and working out to the ends until you have a strand of dough 1 to 1½ in [2.5 to 4 cm] in diameter and 18 in [46 cm] long, tapering the ends slightly. Pinch together all six strands at one end and arrange so the pinched end is at the top of your work space. Fan out the strands so the bottom ends are closest to you.

Cross the outermost right strand all the way over to the left so that it becomes the outermost left strand. Cross what was the outermost left strand all the way over to the right so that it is now the outermost right strand. At this point you have crossed the right to left and left to right positions and have four strands in the middle. Next, take what is now the left outermost strand and cross it over to the middle of the four strands. Take the second-to-right strand and cross it over so that it becomes the outermost left strand. Take the outermost right strand and cross it over to the middle of the four middle strands, then cross the second-to-left strand all the way over to the right so that it becomes the outermost right strand. Repeat this pattern, alternating sides (outermost left strand to the middle, second-to-right over to become the outermost left strand, outermost right strand to the middle, second-to-left over to become the outermost right strand, and so on) until the entire loaf is braided.

Pinch together the strands at the end of the braid and tuck underneath the loaf. Do the same with the pinched edges at the top. Carefully place the braided loaf in the middle of the parchment-lined baking pan.

To braid two three-strand challahs, take three of the logs and roll them out into tapered strands, as described previously. Pinch together the three strands at one end and arrange so the pinched end is at the top of your work space. Fan out the strands so the bottom ends are closest to you.

Braid the strands tightly, as if you were braiding hair. Pinch together the strands at the end of the braid and tuck underneath the loaf. Do the same with the pinched edges at the top. Repeat with the three remaining pieces of dough to form a second braided loaf. Carefully place both braided loaves on the parchment-lined baking pan, maximizing the amount of space around each loaf.

To make the egg wash, whisk the egg in a small bowl. Brush it on the braided dough, reserving the leftover egg. Cover the pan with oiled plastic wrap and let the dough rise again for 45 minutes to 1 hour, until the loaves have doubled in size and wobble when the pan is shaken. When poked with a finger, the dough should spring back slightly, but an indentation should remain.

Preheat the oven to 375°F [190°C]. Brush the loaf again with a thin layer of the egg wash, and sprinkle with the sesame seeds and poppy seeds.

Bake until a golden brown crust has formed on the outside, about 25 minutes for the smaller loaves and 30 minutes for the larger one, rotating the pan halfway through baking. The loaf should sound hollow when tapped gently on the bottom with your knuckles. Let cool on wire racks.

Enjoy warm, or store in a resealable plastic bag at room temperature for up to 5 days.

Strawberry Challah "Shortcake"

Serves 4

We make this at the deli, and it's a winner. Our challah serves as the "cake" since it's rich and sweet. We caramelize the edges so it's also crunchy and buttery. Don't let the number of steps deter you; these shortcakes are easy and come together quickly!

Take out **½ cup [110 g] of butter** from your refrigerator and let it soften. Hull and quarter **8 oz [230 g] strawberries**, or substitute an equal amount of blueberries, blackberries, or raspberries. Plop them into a bowl and toss with a **few heavy pinches of sugar**. Let 'em sit for 10 minutes. Slice **4 slices of challah**, about 1 in [2.5 cm] thick. Cut off the crusts, then shmear the butter on both sides of the bread. Sprinkle heavily with sugar.

Heat a cast-iron skillet over medium heat, and sear the challah slices, in batches, on both sides until golden brown. They're going to smell rich, sweet, and caramelized—that's how you know they're ready. You could whip up **some heavy cream**, and get real fancy and add a little **sour cream** and **confectioners' sugar**. Or you could use that Cool Whip that's been hanging out in your freezer since Thanksgiving or an aerosol whipped cream. Vanilla ice cream works, too.

Layer the golden, crunchy challah slices, the berries, and whatever creamy topping you choose on a platter from your finest china. Serve **maple syrup** on the side if you want to gild the lily.

Challah Onion Rolls

Makes 12 rolls

Our ode to the onion rolls at Wolfie Cohen's Rascal House. Soft and squishy, these will definitely fit in your purse.

Prepare **challah dough** through the second rise. Sauté **1 chopped medium yellow onion** in **olive oil** seasoned with a little **salt** in a skillet over medium heat until soft and translucent, but not brown. Set aside to cool. In a small bowl, mix together **1 Tbsp of garlic powder** and **1 tsp of onion powder**. Line a baking sheet with parchment paper.

Punch down the dough, remove it from the bowl, and place it on a countertop. Separate it into twelve equal pieces. Sprinkle each piece with 1 tsp of the garlic-onion powder, turning over to coat both sides. Make sure the dough is completely covered. Sprinkle a little of the reserved powder mixture onto your countertop, and roll one piece of dough into a strand about 12 in [30.5 cm] long. Tie into a knot, crossing one end over and pulling it gently through, and then pinch the ends of the strands together to create a roll. Place seam-side down on a parchment-lined baking sheet. Repeat with all of the dough to create twelve rolls. Space evenly on the baking sheet. Allow the rolls to rise for 1 hour, covered loosely with a clean kitchen towel. While the dough rises, preheat the oven to 375°F.

Brush the tops of the rolls with two coats of **egg wash** and then spoon equal portions of the onion mixture into the center of each roll, making a well with the back of your spoon and your fingers. It's OK if the onions spill out of the center and onto the edge of the roll—this will create a tasty, soft, oniony middle and a more charred onion exterior. Sprinkle each roll with **poppy or sesame seeds**, or both. Bake for 20 minutes or until golden brown, cool on a wire baking rack, and serve.

It's Sukkot Season, Mother#$@#ers

Harvest Partying

Historically, Jews were tailors and merchants, lawyers and moneylenders, dentists, and doctors. Farmers? Working the land? With our bare hands? Not so much. Not since the seventh century or so. And, in more modern times, not unless you live on an Israeli kibbutz or quit med school to milk cows, or, say, leave the *Daily Show* to run a forty-five-acre animal sanctuary in Upstate New York, and the accompanying Instagram account called "the Daily Squeal," with your wife.

For thousands of years, Jews have had their own form of barn raising, of harvest partying, of celebrating the agricultural cycle and honoring crops. By eating them beneath a full moon, huddled happily inside ephemeral huts made of bamboo poles or pine boards, which we, notoriously unhandy Jews, actually built ourselves.

Sukkot is quietly turning into a bit of a mini–Jewish Burning Man. The simple, three-sided structures have traditionally been decorated with hanging corn and cranberries, baskets brimming with apples and pears, and Christmas bulbs bought on sale in January. Increasingly, in cities around the world, these open-air sukkahs have become architecturally driven designs to ogle. Creativity is key. Competition is stiff.

It started in 2010, with "Sukkah City," in New York, where some 600 artists and architects from forty-something countries submitted sukkahs of all shapes and sizes and materials, from which critics selected a dozen for interactive display in Union Square. There was Dwell's Sukkah Project, in Dallas. Something called Sukkahville, in Toronto. Detroit, too, turned its Capitol Park into a playground of high-concept (yet still rabbi-certified!) sukkahs: one fashioned from recycled vegetable crates aglow with purple LED lights, another built to resemble a pine cone. There are sukkahs built out of street-sourced cardboard, birch bark and moss, and mirrors. There are sukkahs set with long, elaborate, candelabra-topped tables. Sukkahs with Wi-Fi and DJs and baristas serving almond milk lattes.

Sukkot is on its way to becoming fall's most festive Jewish event (following its most sober: Yom Kippur, five days before it). You could host a five-course farm-to-sukkah supper for 150 at $150 a head, like some chefs have done. Or just roast some squash, stuff some knishes, roll in a keg of seasonal craft beer, and call it a sukkah party. Sukkah hopping! It's catching on. There's even an app for that: Open Sukkah, launched by Toronto–turned–Tel Aviv resident Aaron Taylor. His goal is to create a global sukkah map, so everyone—from Budapest to Buenos Aires to Boston—seeking a sukkah can find one.

It's all a far cry from the bare-bones lean-tos of Jews' nomadic desert days, and yet the spirit of the sukkah remains the same. The notion of a temporary dwelling, open to all, has taken on new relevance in the twenty-first century, with the rise in the number of homeless people and refugees and families forced to flee in the face of raging wildfires. It's a symbol of the fact that home—for too many—is still something impermanent. For one week every fall, Sukkot reminds us that what matters is food and shelter, family and friends; that life, like a sukkah, is fragile and fleeting, yet also fun.

Dear Wise Sons,
What the heck are a lulav and an etrog and do I really need them to celebrate Sukkot?

Sincerely,
Lazy-but-Sukkot-Loving Jew

Dear Lazy Jew,
Only if you want to be legit. An etrog is a yellow citron that looks like an extra-large lemon with a bad case of acne. It tastes floral, a bit bitter. A lulav is a closed palm frond from a date tree, bound with myrtle and willows. You won't find this little Judaica bundle at Whole Foods— they're still reeling from that matzo-display-at-Hanukkah faux pas. You can buy one on Amazon, starting around forty bucks. That's a steal, really, as a single unblemished etrog from Calabria was recently going for $500. A couple of California farmers actually grow them, too. Otherwise, with apologies to the rabbi, we say a lemon, plucked from a tree in the backyard, will have to do.

Love,
Wise Sons

Not a Lower East Side Knish

Makes 5 to 8 knishes

Second only to "Pigs" in Blankets (page 68), I love a good knish—especially our roti knish: creamy-savory potato filling encased in a thin layer of ultraflaky dough. It is the perfect finger food. Using sheets of store-bought premade roti dough helps you knock these babies out fast. (Frozen roti dough is available at some grocery chains and most Asian markets.)

For the filling, cook about **1 lb [455 g] of peeled russet potatoes** in generously salted boiling water until soft, maybe 20 to 25 minutes. Drain and transfer to the bowl of your stand mixer. Add about **1 diced and well-caramelized yellow onion**, **2 tsp of kosher salt**, a **pinch of black pepper**, and **2 heaping spoons of softened cream cheese** to the bowl. (A whisk and a large bowl work, too, if you're analog.) Begin mixing at low speed and gradually increase the speed to medium. (The filling will taste a little salty at this point.)

Work in batches while keeping the rest of the roti in the freezer. Let **5 roti** defrost slightly on the counter for about 30 minutes. Plop a generous portion of filling in the middle of each one. Fold the dough over the filling to make a half-moon, push out the air, and crimp the edges tight. Sprinkle and press some **sesame seeds** over the top of the pocket if you like. Score the top a few times so it doesn't pop open. Chill in the refrigerator while you fill the remaining roti. (At this point you can freeze the knishes in resealable plastic bags for up to 3 months.) Fry in **vegetable oil** until they're beautifully golden. Sprinkle with salt and don't forget the **deli mustard** for dipping.

BRUNCH

Bringing home the bagels

Why Wait So Long on the Sidewalk?

Jews used to eat breakfast: bagels and lox; lox, onions, and eggs; Entenmann's crumb cake; a carton of Tropicana, of course. We'd gather in the kitchen around the Formica-topped table, maybe the dining room if we were getting fancy. It was mostly a family affair, and most definitely a morning affair. "Grandma didn't wait until noon to eat, she ate at 7:00 a.m.," as Evan puts it. It was also, above all, an at-home affair.

We're not sure where, exactly, the late-morn sidewalk swarms first started. Likely on New York's Upper West Side at Barney Greengrass, in the '80s. Or a few blocks south at Sarabeth's. "I was the original brunch girl," owner Sara Levine (Jew!) once claimed. Then came the gaggles of gays gathering for eggs in Greenwich Village and soon *Sex and the City*. Clearly, Carrie and friends commiserating with mimosas over Manhattan men contributed to the craze that has been, and continues to be, brunch.

The word was first introduced back in 1895 by a Brit named Guy Beringer, who wrote a piece entitled "Brunch: A Plea" for *The Hunter's Weekly*. He called for the end of England's postchurch tradition of an early, heavy Sunday dinner—and for a heretical midday blend of breakfast and lunch instead. Among his convincing arguments: "It renders early rising not only unnecessary but ridiculous. You get up when the world is warm, or at least, when it is not so cold. You are, therefore, able to prolong your Saturday nights."

He also adds prophetically, "P.S.—Beer and whiskey are admitted as substitutes for tea and coffee." Today, pricey cocktails are, too. (It's 11:00 a.m. somewhere!)

Brunch has morphed into the much-loved, most-mocked, most social meal of the weekend, commanding wait times worthy of a bad layover. Diners devour it, but chefs will tell you: They despise brunch. Most only do it because—bottomless mimosa-line—it's a moneymaker. Oh, what people are willing to pay for someone else to poach their eggs.

Here's a brilliant, perhaps old-fashioned idea, a blast from our grandparents' past: How about hosting friends at home? During daylight hours. You know, welcoming guests upon arrival, inviting them inside to kick off their shoes, lounge around your living room or sun-drenched backyard or even your messy, wobbly kitchen table to enjoy bagels and lox, babka and Bloodys, and most importantly, each other. After all, the ultimate point of this modern-day, midmorn meal dubbed "brunch" is to wake up and break bread with the people we love—not to squander half a day leaning against a parking meter, hoping to hear our name being called.

Doesn't have to be elegant, as Evan knows firsthand. His Nana Goldie, in Palm Springs, would defrost a dozen bagels from her freezer, then head out to Jensen's Finest Foods for all the accoutrements. She'd come home, unwrap the wax paper, and unceremoniously plop a bunch of sturgeon and salmon on her Lucite table, along with a block or two of foil-wrapped Philadelphia cream cheese. There was always a bowl of purple grapes. (Ice-cold, of course. Everyone knows they taste better that way.) Sometimes she'd pluck a few oranges from her tree to squeeze fresh OJ. Grapefruits, too, always accompanied by her stash of serrated, sharp-toothed spoons.

Then family would trickle in—uncles, aunts, cousins, some arriving via golf cart, others by Buick, all snowbirds with funny accents fleeing the Canadian cold. Inside, the AC would be blasting, the gossip going ("So-and-so got into Harvard . . . "); the questions flowing ("What's on *60 Minutes* tonight?"), the medical questions coming, like rapid fire, at Evan's dad the doctor ("Stu, you think I need surgery?" "What do I do about my aching balls?"). Evan and his brother would lounge around the shag carpet, eating, listening, and by osmosis, learning what it is to be a Jew.

The Ideal Brunch Spread

1. OJ + bubbly: Fresh squeezed with corner-store sparkling wine.

2. Grapefruits (halved) **with grapefruit spoons:** The most underrated utensil.

3. Bagels: Figure a dozen for every ten people or so. (Somebody, carbs be damned, inevitably downs two.) As for the mix, best to double down on "everything" and "plain"— they're always the two most popular. Poppy, sesame, of course. Salt? Sure, one, maybe two, tops. "But, please, don't even consider cinnamon raisin," says Evan. "They're not bagels."

4. Capers: The small nonpareils are best.

5. Lemon wedges: For a quick spritz.

6. Other accoutrements: Red onion, sliced tomatoes, sliced cucumber, sliced radish.

7. Soft-boiled eggs: Just because. Sprinkled with flaky sea salt and cracked black pepper.

8. Greens: Such as arugula mixed with sprouts and fresh herbs, because you're a hippie at heart.

9. Smoked Fish Salad: Mmm... (page 180).

10. Olives: On the side, like a garnish. Not those canned sliced black olives—whole plump Greek olives only!

11. Avocado: Fork mashed with a dash of olive oil. Makes a good dairy-free alternative to cream cheese, too.

12. Purple grapes: Ice-cold!

13. The Goldie: (Page 113.)

14. Shmear: Philadelphia is the tried-and-true store-bought brand, and our love for it is true. All of Wise Sons' shmears start with a Philadelphia base. The organic stuff, making our own—nothing came close. Also, a shmear must shmear both halves of the bagel, please.

15. Smoked salmon: With fresh dill.

16. Pickles: It's not a Jewish meal without them!

17. Coffee: It matters.

The Go-To Guide to All Kinds of Shmears

Making a good shmear is easy. Start with a softened brick of cream cheese—the ones wrapped in foil—and a sturdy stand mixer. The trick is to let the mixer go for a few minutes on high. That's it. For the best plain whipped cream cheese, add a splash of milk or cream.

Scallion (Not Chive)
Lots of thinly sliced white and green scallions

Roasted Scallion
Charred scallions, a pinch of grated lemon zest, a squeeze of juice, kosher salt

Kimchi
Puréed and drained kimchi, a splash of sriracha or sambal

New Nova
Bits of Nova, a dollop of prepared horseradish, chopped fresh dill

Dad's Favorite
A glug of maple syrup, a small handful of chopped toasted walnuts

Sweet Cream
Jam of your choice, a few big pinches of sugar, a bit of grated lemon zest

Honey-Jalapeño
Sliced jalapeños (seeded or not), lots of honey, cracked black pepper

Kinda Spicy
Harissa paste, a squeeze of lemon juice

Pimento Dip
Shredded Cheddar cheese, a big pinch of brown sugar, chopped pimento, a dash of Worcestershire, hot sauce

Loaded Baked Potato
Shredded Cheddar cheese, thinly sliced scallion, crispy pastrami bits, cracked black pepper

Fruits-to-Nuts
Chopped apricots, honey, grated orange zest, chopped toasted pistachios

Birthday Cake
Rainbow sprinkles, a lot of sugar, pinch of salt

To Toast or Not Toast or Double-Toast?

That is the question.

And the correct answer is: Toasting always tastes better. Unless you just pulled a bagel out of the wood-burning oven at St-Viateur, in Montreal, a just-baked bagel deserves to be toasted. Don't be afraid to go a shade darker, either. Sesame seeds get nutty, onions get caramelized. Toasting improves the depth and texture of a day-old bagel. Supermarket bagels? Definite toast situation. As a general rule, it's wise to demand double-toasting at airports, Disneyland, and wherever bad bagels are found.

The L Word

I once witnessed what looked like a drug deal at a Yom Kippur break-the-fast.

"Hey, do you have any pills?" one middle-aged Jewish man asked another.

"Yeah, I got some," he replied, dipping his hand into his pants pocket. He pulled out a little white capsule and quietly palmed it to his friend.

"What is that?" I whispered. Were they trying to liven up the six o'clock bagel buffet with something illicit?

"Lactaid," they replied, looking at me, like, duh.

Ah, right. As a rare pizza-quesadilla-cheese-chowing Jew who downs milkshakes like water with nary a stomach gurgle, I forgot: Jews are among the most lactose-intolerant people in the world. (Rather ironic we come from the Land of Milk and Honey, isn't it?)

Studies show that 60 to 80 percent of Jews, be they Sephardic or Ashkenazi, are lactose intolerant, outranked only by East Asians, Central Asians, and Africans. (Fun, but not surprising fact: Denmark and Ireland tie for most lactose-tolerant country in the world.) Lactose intolerance is yet another reason why, as Jennifer 8. Lee puts it: "Chow mein is the chosen food of the Chosen People." (See pages 79 and 86 for Christmas Dinner and Sunday Night Takeout.)

Shmear v. Cream Cheese

Is it Cream Cheese or Shmear? We called in an actual cream cheese expert—Rabbi Jeffery A. Marx of the Santa Monica Synagogue—to settle the debate once and for all.

I say "cream cheese," Evan says "shmear"—which means Wise Sons says "shmear." Maybe it's an East Coast–West Coast thing?

We rang up a real-live cream cheese expert, Rabbi Jeffrey A. Marx, of Santa Monica Synagogue—who has written extensively about bagels and cream cheese in Jewish America—to settle this very important semantics debate.

"Cream cheese has never been called anything but cream cheese in America," he declares. Ever since the nineteenth century, when early Dutch and English settlers combined milk and cream and dubbed it such. Soon dairy farmers around the Philadelphia area began producing it in small quantities. And once trains started chugging, cream cheese came to New York City, just as Eastern European Jews started arriving.

Shmear is Yiddish for "spread," explains Marx. Originally it was a verb, meaning "to spread." In America, only butter and chicken fat were shmeared on bread. It wasn't until the late 1920s, once cream cheese became more affordable and available, that it, too, was shmeared on bread, and soon, bagels, by the Jewish community.

"Probably, not until, at the earliest, the 1940s, in delis, was the term 'a shmear' used to refer to cream cheese," says Marx. "And even then, it referred to spreading (usually a bagel) with cream cheese. As in the call to the kitchen 'one bagel with a shmear!'" But "shmear" was never used to refer to cream cheese per se, he says. As in, "Go to the store and buy a shmear."

Wise Sons uses shmear as a noun and a verb. But the New England native in me will defer to Marx: "Originally, cream cheese was always, always called cream cheese."

 Spread your cream cheese—or shmear your shmear—with care. Go "coast to coast," as Evan says, with a steady hand to ensure an even thickness. The pros use an actual spreader, but the back of a spoon works well. Better than a butter knife, even.

The Smoking Section

If you only go with one, it's got to be the classic: smoked salmon or lox. (The word "lox" comes from the Yiddish *laks*, itself based on the German word for salmon, *lachs*.) What's the difference between smoked salmon and lox? Lox is basically just salmon that's been cured and brined, but not smoked. Allow 2 to 3 oz [55 to 85 g] per person.

A lot of grocery stores these days carry good stuff (like Acme Smoked Fish, for example). Sounds crazy, but forgo wild for farmed, which is consistently fatty. Wild tends to be too lean and dry, and bagels beg for luxurious fish. "Hate to say it, but here's where the more you spend, the better quality fish you get," says Evan. Here's a breakdown of what's behind the deli counter.

Lox
Old-school fatty, silky, salty, and brine-cured, but not smoked. Belly lox is the best.

Gravlax
Scandinavian-style salmon cured with a little salt, dill, lemon, and vodka or gin or aquavit. It is not smoked (see recipe on page 142).

Pastrami-rubbed salmon
Rubbed with pepper and coriander before being hot- or cold-smoked. Peppery, flavorful, and smoky.

Cold-smoked salmon or Nova
A whole side of salmon cured or dry-brined in salt and sugar, and then cold-smoked over wood.

Hot-smoked whitefish or trout
Mild, sweet, smoky, and flaky.

Smoked sable
Buttery, sweet, paprika-tinged, and smoked.

Sturgeon
Earthy, fishy, and superfatty, it's the most luxurious smoked fish in the deli.

Herring
Old Jewish men's favorite omega-3s, cured, pickled in a vinegary brine, or dunked in sour cream, which I can still see, creamy white, dripping from my grandfather's fork, and chin.

Kippered salmon
Cured, then hot-smoked. Luscious.

DIY Cured Fish

Serves 4 to 6

CURED FISH

1 Tbsp Diamond Crystal kosher salt

1 Tbsp sugar

½ tsp freshly ground black pepper

Grated zest of 1 lemon

8 oz [225 g] skin-on salmon or sturgeon fillet (look for a fatty, well-marbled piece)

1½ tsp vodka

3 or 4 dill sprigs, plus 2 Tbsp chopped fresh dill for later

MUSTARD SAUCE

¼ cup plus 2 Tbsp [90 ml] olive oil

2 Tbsp brown deli mustard, such as Gulden's

2 Tbsp distilled white vinegar

1 Tbsp sugar

1 Tbsp chopped fresh dill

Toasted rye bread or bagels for serving

To make the cured fish, in a medium bowl, mix together the salt, sugar, pepper, and lemon zest and set aside.

Rinse the fish well under cold running water, and pat it dry with a few paper towels. Place the fish in the bowl of seasoning and turn to coat it on all sides, making sure to use all of the seasoning.

This recipe is simple yet impressive. Save any leftover mustard sauce to use as a light salad dressing.

Put the fish in a 1 gal [3.8 L] resealable plastic bag and add the vodka and dill sprigs. Use your hands to massage the bag lightly to distribute the liquid. Carefully press out the air from the bag and seal. Refrigerate for 3 to 4 days, depending on whether you like a milder or stronger flavor.

Remove the fish from the bag and rinse in cold running water to remove the seasoning, and pat with paper towels until completely dry. Put the chopped dill in a shallow bowl and turn the salmon through the dill to completely and evenly coat.

To make the mustard sauce, mix all the ingredients together in a small bowl. The mustard sauce will keep in an airtight container in the refrigerator for up to 5 days. Makes ¾ cup [175 ml].

Slice the salmon thinly, drizzle with the mustard sauce, and serve with toasted bread or bagels. The fish will keep tightly wrapped in plastic in the refrigerator for up to 3 days.

 The key to building a better bagel sandwich? Ratios. Resist the urge to pile on mountains of smoked salmon. Think about complementary ingredients: You want the right mix of creamy, salty, fatty, tart, and crunchy. Don't bury the bagel—balance it, be it open-faced or closed. Which is yet another hot debate . . . I say open-faced. Evan likes closed, for practical purposes.

The Big Bacon Debate

Rachel: "What about including bacon in the book? It's Jews' gateway pig! It could be fun to do something, like . . . 'My First Bacon,' with recipes where we, like, sneak in bacon, but it's not the star?"

Evan: "I dunno. The deli's not kosher, but we drew the line at pork and shellfish. We don't serve it. I'm not sure about having a pork page."

Rachel: "Yeah, OK. What about how some Jews refuse to make it at home, but will totally order it when they go out? Favorite breakfast spots for bacon?"

Evan: "Maybe we just say, 'Pork' and leave the page blank?"

Rachel: "Or maybe it just says, 'Call Michael Solomonov'? He didn't try bacon until he was twenty."

[Pause. Suddenly craving a corned pork belly Reuben.]

Rachel: "Or what about a plug for 'cultured meat'? You know, the idea of pork being grown in labs from animal cells—no 'dirty pig' or unclean cloven hooves and all. What about kosher bacon? It's going to be big."

Evan: "But will it be good?"

Rachel: "It definitely won't be as *good*."

Evan's older brother Ari: "No pork."

Rosh Hashana

How 'bout them apples & honey?

Why the Jewish New Year Is the Best New Year

For starters, it doesn't kick off with a serious hangover.

It also doesn't come with all the pressures and decisions of December 31. Like, What should we do? Where should we go? What should I wear? Who am I going to kiss? Do we really want to do a ten-course supper plus Champagne toast at midnight for $255 per person? (No, we don't.) Meanwhile, Uber rates are surging. Airports are packed. The weather typically sucks. And if you stay home alone with Ryan Seacrest or Kathy Griffin, watching the ball drop in Times Square, you're depressed.

The Jewish New Year, on the other hand, is a (mostly) joyous, low-key occasion that just kind of creeps up on you one gorgeous September day. Like fall leaves or the new season of *SNL*. It's festive, but not *that* festive.

Rosh Hashana comes with very few expectations. Well, other than our parents' expectations—they call to tell us to go to temple, which we may or may not do. (And feel guilty when we don't. But we *will* go on Yom Kippur, see page 176.) At night, on Rosh Hashana, affordable Ubers abound if we need them, but we usually don't, because we're cozy at home, hanging in our slippers with family and friends, dipping apples in honey. Some Jews might go apple picking or make a special pilgrimage to the farmers' market in honor of what, we hope, will be a sweet year.

Otherwise, if we go anywhere, it's to the beach—for Tashlich, with a bottle of rosé, maybe a cheese board, and a bag of birdseed (bread crumbs are so 5778). And as the sun sets, and the seagulls squawk, we toss our sins into the sea with the rest of our tribe. It's our casual, carefree California way of casting off the ills of the past year—and ushering in the next. No confetti or bubbly flutes or resolutions to join CrossFit required.

Fall Vegetable Hash

Serves 4

VEGETABLE HASH

8 oz [225 g] russet potatoes, cut into ½ in [12 mm] cubes

4 Tbsp [60 ml] vegetable oil

8 oz [225 g] delicata squash, halved, seeded, and sliced into ¼ in [6 mm] thick half-moons

5 oz [140 g] Brussels sprouts, thinly sliced

5 scallions, ends trimmed, cut into 1 in [2.5 cm] lengths, plus thinly sliced scallions for serving

1½ tsp Diamond Crystal kosher salt

Toasted pepitas (pumpkin seeds) for serving

Freshly ground black pepper

WHOLE-GRAIN MAPLE MUSTARD

2 Tbsp maple syrup

2 Tbsp whole-grain Dijon mustard

To make the hash, preheat the oven to 450°F [230°C].

Bring a medium pot of salted water to a boil over medium-high heat. Add the potatoes and cook until just tender, but not falling apart, 5 to 6 minutes. Drain and set aside.

Coat a large cast-iron skillet or Dutch oven with 1 Tbsp of the vegetable oil and heat over medium-high until shimmering.

A most versatile dish, this makes a great side for a meal at home, or double the recipe for a potluck. Serve it for breakfast with sunny-side-up eggs and rye toast as an alternative to corned beef hash, as we do at our deli. Or top it with the maple mustard for an extra sweet New Year.

Meanwhile, in a large bowl, combine the cooked potatoes, the squash, Brussels sprouts, and scallions. Toss with the salt and the remaining 3 Tbsp of vegetable oil to coat well.

Add the contents of the bowl to the hot pan in one even layer and cook, undisturbed, for about 5 minutes. The vegetables will begin to form a crispy crust on the bottom and smell toasty, but not burned. Continue to cook, gently folding the vegetables together occasionally so they begin to brown on all sides, 5 to 8 minutes more. Place the pan in the oven for 10 minutes so the vegetables continue to brown.

To make the mustard, in a small bowl, whisk together the maple syrup and mustard until well blended.

Remove the vegetables from the oven, and serve immediately, topped with the toasted pepitas, a drizzle of the maple mustard, the thinly sliced scallions, and a few grinds of pepper. Store leftover mustard in an airtight container in the refrigerator for up to 1 month.

Honey Cake from the Box

Serves 8 to 10

CAKE

One 15¼ oz [432 g] box vanilla cake mix (we like Betty Crocker Super Moist French Vanilla)

2 tsp ground cinnamon

1 tsp Diamond Crystal kosher salt

½ tsp ground allspice

1 cup [340 g] honey

¾ cup [180 ml] vegetable oil

¼ cup [60 ml] fresh orange juice (from about 1 to 1½ large navel oranges)

¼ cup [60 ml] whiskey

4 large eggs

GLAZE

½ cup [60 g] confectioners' sugar

1 Tbsp plus 1 tsp whole milk

½ teaspoon vanilla extract

It might be a classic, but making honey cake is a pain in the ass. (Unless you make this one.) I have no qualms about Betty Crocker. (Not a Jew. Not even a real person!) Since 1921, her (its) boxed vanilla cake mix has wowed guests and saved gobs of time. Coupled with fall spices and spoonfuls of honey, it makes a mean last-minute honey cake.

To make the cake, preheat the oven to 350°F [180°C]. Generously grease a 10 in [25 cm] nonstick tube pan with cooking spray or vegetable oil.

In a large bowl, whisk together the cake mix, cinnamon, salt, and allspice. Make a well in the center and add the honey, oil, orange juice, and whiskey. Crack the eggs into the well. Whisk together, scraping the bottom and sides of the bowl to ensure the batter is smooth.

Pour the batter into the prepared tube pan and bake until the center of the cake springs back when touched, about 45 minutes.

Cool in the pan on a wire rack. Use a knife to gently separate the sides of the cake from the sides of the pan, and sit the pan on top of a whiskey bottle or wine bottle. Press down on the sides of the pan to remove it. Place the cake on the counter and use a knife to separate the bottom and inside ring of the cake from the pan. Flip the cake upside down onto the palm of your hand or a large piece of parchment paper on your countertop, and then flip right-side up onto a cake stand or plate.

Reduce the oven temperature to 200°F [95°C].

To make the glaze, mix together the confectioners' sugar, milk, and vanilla in a small bowl to make a loose paste. Use the back of a spoon or an offset spatula to spread the glaze over the top of the cake. Place in the warm oven for 4 to 5 minutes to set the glaze.

This cake will keep at room temperature, wrapped well in plastic wrap, for 1 week.

Challah Apple Fritter Monkey Bread

Makes 1 loaf

1 recipe challah dough (page 125)

1 Tbsp unsalted butter

1½ lb [455 g] Granny Smith apples or other good baking apples, peeled, cored, and cut into ¼ in [6 mm] pieces

2 Tbsp granulated sugar

½ tsp Diamond kosher salt

2½ tsp ground cinnamon

1 Tbsp fresh lemon juice

1 Tbsp all-purpose flour

1 cup [200 g] packed light brown sugar

½ cup [110 g] unsalted butter, melted

1 recipe Glaze (optional, page 153)

Preheat the oven to 350°F [180°C]. Grease a twelve-cup Bundt pan with nonstick cooking spray and line a rimmed baking sheet with parchment paper.

Prepare the challah dough to the second rise. During the second rise, prepare the apple filling. Combine the butter, apples, granulated sugar, and salt in a nonstick skillet. Cook over medium heat until the apples are soft but not completely broken down, about 5 minutes. Add ½ tsp of the cinnamon and the lemon juice and cook for 1 to 2 minutes more. Stir in the flour and cook for 1 minute more. Remove from the heat and let cool.

Mix the brown sugar and the remaining 2 tsp of cinnamon together in a small bowl.

Punch down the dough and turn it out onto a lightly floured surface. Divide into 4 equal pieces. Working with 1 piece at a time, divide into 4 pieces, then quarter each of these. Repeat with the remaining dough. You will have 64 pieces in total.

Working with 1 piece of dough at a time, use your fingers to flatten each into a 2 in [5 cm] round. Place 1 tsp of filling in the middle of the dough, brush along the edge with the melted butter, and stretch one edge over the filling. Fold in the other edges to make a sealed packet. Repeat with the remaining dough pieces.

Dip each packet of dough in the butter, then into the cinnamon-sugar mixture. Place in the prepared pan. Repeat with the remaining dough, pressing the balls snugly into the pan. Cover with a clean towel and set in a warm place to rise for 1 hour.

Transfer the pan to the prepared baking sheet and bake until the top is a deep golden brown, with bubbling at the edges, about 45 minutes.

Cool in the pan for 20 minutes, then carefully run a knife around the edges to loosen. Turn the bread out onto a platter or cake stand and cool for 10 minutes more. Drizzle with the glaze, if desired, and serve warm.

How to Blow a Shofar like a Billionaire

It turns out, some of the leading tech CEOs of our time are quite skilled in the most analog of instruments.

Last fall, as I wrote in the *New York Times*, the founder of Facebook (and Wise Sons customer) posted a video of himself, on Facebook, tooting his own ram's horn in the comfort of his living room. "Mark Zuckerberg is celebrating Rosh Hashana," read the status update, complete with an apple-and-honey emoji. With chest and cheeks full, he blew an impressive *tekiah-teruah-shevarim*, as good as any rabbi's, racking up more than a million likes. (Although an earlier post of his baby goat standing on top of a tortoise got more.)

"Love the Jewish pride!" one commenter wrote. "That's some serious blowing skills."

Four rabbi-approved tips for getting started:

1. Pretend it's a trumpet.

2. Put on some Chapstick for a strong seal around the mouthpiece, keeping your lower lip loose.

3. Take a deep breath and blow, vibrating your lips like a kid giving a raspberry

4. Practice. (Like your parents made you do on the piano.)

THE ALL-GROWN-UP YEARS

Passover
Let my people eat

Confessions of a First-Time Seder Host

If having a bar or bat mitzvah means you're becoming a Jewish adult, hosting your first Seder means you're becoming your Jewish mother. Or at least a mature Jewish adult who understands the importance of carrying on tradition. Of telling, and retelling, the Passover story, of our days as slaves, of our exodus from ancient Egypt, and of our celebration of freedom. Of the holiday's worldwide relevance today, when people, too many people, still face oppression, 3,000 years later.

Some host their first Seder after they buy their first house, or have their first child. Others, away at school and homesick for the holidays, start early. Like Evan and his friend and future business partner, Leo—two nice, not-yet-mature dudes who decided, at UC Berkeley, to throw a Seder-slash-dinner-party for forty or so friends.

"I don't really remember it," says Evan of the event on Regent Street. Clearly, more than the requisite four glasses of wine were consumed. No, not Manischewitz—they had better taste than that. Charles Shaw. Two-Buck Chuck. By the case. In red Solo cups. (College!)

Looking back at photos and a video of the occasion, though, jogged his memory. There were wobbly tables and plastic utensils, flimsy chairs on loan from Berkeley Hillel and Craigslist couches pushed together. The Seder plate was spare, and paper, but, hey, at least there was one—topped with a chicken bone, sucked clean; a single egg that may or may not have been hard-boiled; and a scrap of notebook paper scrawled with the phrase "bitter herb" in lieu of a leaf of romaine. Dread-locked Leo, true to form, wore not a yarmulke but a Rasta-style hat. Evan cooked a brisket. And at least one goy-guest brought a challah. (Someone always does.*) "Dayenu" was sung with gusto. And the second half of the Seder, après-afikomen, likely never happened. Still, a good Jewish time was clearly had by all—as evidenced by the carpets and walls, which, they discovered the next hungover morning, were covered in red wine. Elijah must've gone rogue.

Of course, as the host grows up, so does the Seder. After college, "Friendsover," like "Friendsgiving," becomes a tradition in its own right. An invitation extended, from some good soul, to wandering Jews. Those far from home, struggling to make overpriced rents, in cities around the country, where they are left to flail around in religion, as in life, and figure out what they'd like to uniquely do with it.

In Evan and Leo's case, they just kept cooking. Until, in 2011, they did something pretty unheard of at the time. As cofounders of the country's first pop-up Jewish deli, they took Passover public. They sold tickets. To strangers. To a Seder. For real money. And those tickets sold out. It was a sold-out Seder! With really good food: pickled Bull's Blood beets and hand-grated, fluorescent-fuchsia horseradish. Clean, flavorful broth buoying matzo balls as God intended them to be: featherlight and fluffy. Peppery-sweet, fork-tender brisket. And, yes, even the gefilte fish: a custom grind of rock cod and whitefish in a fennel-thyme fumet. It was a far cry from the jars of congealed liquid that line the shelves at Safeway every season—and anything but the snoozy, stilted Seders of my youth.

As much as I'd give to be able to gather around my grandparents' dining room table today, I didn't appreciate it at the time. I'd sit there, in my skirt and saggy tights, picking at sprigs of parsley, sort of listening—and starving—until Grandma's tough, gray brisket was served.

At this Seder, there were no loud, lengthy conversations about what route everyone took to get there; no cranky aunts chastising me for sneaking a spoonful of charoset too soon; no "help clear the table" mandates from Mom. Just fabulous food, new friends, and a semiprofessional singer, who did the Four Questions justice.

A decade later, Wise Sons' Seder tradition continues. They've since expanded to the Contemporary Jewish Museum, where, every spring, they slave away, slicing brisket for some two hundred people over two nights—and uniting the city's often secular Jewish community around the table, to break blistered, olive-oil-tinged matzo together.

Now a mother myself, with family back East, I've made Passover my own: a San Francisco–style Friendsover with grass-fed beef brisket, California wine, homemade macaroons brought by a Seder-obsessed Presbyterian, and the very same crew who had welcomed me as a young West-wandering Jew with nothing else to do.

The only difference: Now we've got a kids' table.

Gentle reminder, gentiles: Passover is a bread-free holiday. Save the challah for Shabbat dinner.

The Whole Twenty-First-Century Seder Shebang

Today's Seder

Really Good Matzo

Makes 12 matzos

2¼ cups [315 g] all-purpose flour,
plus more as needed

⅓ cup [75 ml] extra-virgin olive oil

½ teaspoon Diamond Crystal kosher salt

½ cup [120 ml] room-temperature water

Fine sea salt for sprinkling

Put a pizza stone on an oven rack (a large baking sheet will do, in a pinch) and preheat the oven to 500°F [260°C] for about 45 minutes. Flour a wooden pizza peel or the back of a cold baking sheet generously.

Combine the flour, oil, and salt in a food processor. With the motor running, slowly add the water. The dough will come together into a soft ball. If it is sticky at all, add more flour, 1 Tbsp at a time.

Divide the dough into twelve portions. Using a floured rolling pin, roll one portion at a time on a well-floured work surface into a round about 8 in [20 cm] in diameter and just thin enough to see through. Lightly sprinkle with sea salt and press in the salt with your hands. Prick the dough all over with a fork (this will prevent the dough from puffing up too much).

Carefully place the dough on the pizza peel or cold baking sheet. Gently slide the dough onto the hot pizza stone and bake until the matzo is a light golden color, crisp on each side, and a bit darker at the edges, 2 to 3 minutes, turning once with a wide spatula for even cooking. Transfer the matzo to a cooling rack. Repeat with the remaining dough.

The matzo will keep, tightly wrapped, at room temperature for up to 2 days.

For a week or so every spring, our friends Blake Joffe and Amy Remsen, of Beauty's Bagel Shop in Oakland, California, break down their kitchen at the end of the day, and then restart it, staying late into the night, to make matzo. Three hundred pounds of it for Passover. What comes out, more than the Talmudically prescribed 18 minutes later, is something you won't find in a standard box of Streit's: flaky, blistered, flavorful matzo. While thousands of years of tradition might call for nothing but flour and water, Beauty's adds two tiny but mighty ingredients: olive oil and salt (kosher, of course). But is the matzo itself kosher? "I don't know," says Joffe. "But I don't care. It tastes good." Amen to that. They sell it at their own shop for twelve dollars per pound [455 g]. "Usually people buy a pound or two [a little less than half a kilo or a kilo], then supplement," he says. "They only want to pay so much for the good stuff." Fair enough: A standard box of cardboard sells for around three bucks.

Blessed be Blake Joffe and Amy Remsen, owners of Beauty's, for granting us this recipe. Be sure to use enough olive oil to make the dough supple and easy to handle.

Charoset

Makes almost 8 cups [2 kg]

¾ cup [115 g] golden or dark raisins, or a mixture

½ cup [120 ml] fresh orange juice

½ cup [120 ml] Manischewitz wine

½ tsp ground cinnamon

2½ lb [1.2 kg] crisp tart apples, peeled, cored, and chopped into ¼ in [6 mm] cubes

¾ cup [150 g] finely chopped toasted walnuts

⅓ cup [65 g] golden brown or dark brown sugar

¼ tsp Diamond Crystal kosher salt

The tastiest item on the Seder plate is also beloved by the bowl. Our charoset is the classic Ashkenazi recipe, upgraded. Marinating the raisins ahead of time adds more depth of flavor, and allows you to bust it out while you're busy preparing the rest of the Passover feast. Just chop up fresh apples when you're ready to go.

In a medium bowl, combine the raisins, orange juice, wine, and ¼ tsp of the cinnamon. Toss well to combine and let the raisins macerate for at least 4 and up to 24 hours.

When ready to make the charoset, combine the apples, walnuts, brown sugar, salt, and remaining ¼ tsp of cinnamon with the macerated raisins in a medium bowl. Let stand for at least 1 hour before serving.

Chopped Liver

Serves 4 to 6

1 lb [455 g] organic chicken livers

1 tsp Diamond Crystal kosher salt

⅛ tsp freshly ground black pepper

2 Tbsp Schmaltz (page 56)

2 medium yellow onions, thinly sliced

2 tsp finely chopped fresh parsley

1 tsp minced garlic

½ tsp finely chopped fresh thyme

1 dried bay leaf

⅛ tsp smoked paprika (also known as pimentón)

2 Tbsp brandy

This is chopped liver for those who think they don't like it, which is a lot of people. Most chopped liver tastes a little like iron, which puts some people off. Ours is made with half caramelized onions—what's not to love? It's perfect with matzo on Passover. Or any time of year. We promise.

Start with the best-quality chicken livers you can find. They'll taste much less iron-y and much more like chicken. Former Wise Sons staffers Blake Joffe and Joe Wolf deserve much of the credit for this sublime version of a Jewish deli classic.

Put the livers in a colander in the sink and rinse with cold running water. Pat dry with a paper towel. Use a small paring knife to trim any visible fat, membrane, and green parts. Set the livers on a large plate or small baking sheet and toss with the salt and pepper to evenly coat.

Heat 1 Tbsp of the schmaltz in a large heavy-bottomed, nonreactive skillet over medium-high heat. When the fat begins to smoke, carefully place the livers in the skillet, spacing them out to encourage browning. The hot fat will splatter, so be careful! Sear the livers for 5 minutes on the first side, then use tongs to flip and cook for 3 minutes more. Check for doneness by piercing with a small knife or skewer. Any liquid should run clear. Remove the livers from the skillet and cool on a clean plate or baking sheet. Turn the heat down to medium.

Add the onions and the remaining 1 Tbsp of schmaltz to the skillet. Sauté the onions until softened and beginning to caramelize, about 10 to 12 minutes, stirring with a wooden spoon to promote even browning and prevent sticking. Add the parsley, garlic, thyme, bay leaf, and paprika and stir well to combine. Cook for 5 minutes more, stirring as needed.

Add the brandy to the skillet carefully, as the alcohol may catch fire. Cook for 5 minutes, stirring occasionally. Remove from the heat and spoon the onion mixture onto a baking sheet or large plate to cool. Discard the bay leaf.

Using a stand mixer fitted with a grinder attachment, slowly grind the livers and the onion mixture into a medium bowl and gently fold to combine. Alternatively, you may finely chop the livers and the onion mixture by hand using a chef's knife or a mezzaluna. Refrigerate before serving for a firmer, creamier texture. The chopped liver will keep in an airtight container in the refrigerator for up to 5 days.

Wise Sons' Brisket

Serves 8 (with plenty of leftovers)

⅓ cup [60 g] spicy brown deli mustard (any mustard will work in a pinch), plus more as needed

4½ Tbsp [45 g] Diamond Crystal kosher salt

1 Tbsp freshly ground black pepper

One 6 to 8 lb [2.7 to 3.6 kg] beef brisket

2 Tbsp vegetable oil

3 cups [720 ml] homemade stock (page 55), low-sodium chicken, beef, or vegetable broth, or water

One 12 oz [360 ml] bottle of beer (something dark and sweet, like a porter) or ½ bottle dry red wine (such as Cabernet or Zinfandel)

5 whole pitted prunes

2 dried bay leaves

1 Tbsp packed dark brown sugar

1 lb [455 g] carrots, peeled and cut into 1 in [2.5 cm] chunks

3 medium yellow onlons, thinly sliced

8 garlic cloves, peeled and smashed with the flat side of a knife

2 to 3 Tbsp unsalted butter (optional)

Mix the mustard, salt, and pepper in a small bowl. Slather all over the brisket and place it on a baking sheet. Let sit, uncovered, in the refrigerator for at least 2 hours or overnight for maximum moistness.

My safta in the kitchen, standing maybe four feet tall, the smell of braising beef in the air, my brisket nostalgia is strong. Every family has their classic recipe—be it some "secret" ingredient like onion soup mix (MSG), Heinz chili sauce, or Coca-Cola. Our recipe recalls my roots, but with added sophistication and technique, rather than brand-name shortcuts.

Start with a good piece of meat. Ask for the flat cut, with an even thickness, end to end, to ensure even cooking. You also want a good fat cap (a nice 1 in [2.5 cm] or so layer of fat blanketing the top of the meat) to keep it tender and juicy as it cooks. We use prunes, lots of onions, and carrots for sweetness. The mustard gives a good acidic balance to the final dish. Don't be scared by the large pile of sliced onions—they'll caramelize and provide body for the gravy. While beer gives the beef a slightly nutty flavor, red wine is also great here, especially for holidays like Passover, where having beer in the house is a shonda. *Cooking the brisket a few days ahead will let the flavors marry and make it even better—it also allows for a quick skim of the excess fat.*

Preheat the oven to 350°F [180°C]. Heat the oil in a Dutch oven or another large heavy-bottomed, ovenproof pot over medium heat until shimmering. Add the brisket and sear until browned on both sides, about 5 to 8 minutes per side. You want a nice golden crust. Transfer to a platter and set aside.

Increase the heat to medium-high, add the stock to the pot, and bring to a simmer, scraping up the browned bits from the bottom of the pot. Add the beer, prunes, bay leaves, and brown sugar. Cook until the sugar has dissolved, stirring if necessary. Remove from the heat.

continued

Return the brisket to the pot, fat-side up, and scatter the carrots around the meat. Blanket the meat with the onions and garlic. Cover the pot tightly with a lid or heavy-duty aluminum foil. Transfer to the oven and braise the brisket for about 3 hours, flipping the brisket every hour. Cook until a fork inserted into the center rotates easily, with just a little resistance, but without tearing the meat to shreds.

Remove the brisket from the pot and use a large, sharp knife to cut the brisket against the grain into ¼ in [6 mm] thick slices. Remove the bay leaves from the pot and discard.

Using an immersion blender directly in the pot, purée the jus and the remaining tender vegetables—this will give the gravy a sweet taste and enough body to slick over the brisket.

(At this point, the brisket and gravy can be transferred to a roasting pan, ready to reheat, with the brisket fanned out and smothered by the gravy. Or store in separate containers. Either way, let cool, cover, and refrigerate overnight. If reheating the brisket straight out of the refrigerator, preheat the oven to 300°F [150°C]. Use a spoon to skim off any fat on the surface of the gravy. Cover tightly with heavy-duty aluminum foil and warm for about 30 minutes, or until heated through.)

In the deli, we like a thicker gravy. To achieve this, transfer half of it to a small heavy-bottomed pot and bring to a medium simmer. Return the sliced brisket to the pot with the remaining gravy and keep warm on a burner at its lowest setting. Cook the gravy in the small pot until reduced by half, 30 to 40 minutes, stirring as needed so it doesn't burn. If you like, whisk in the butter for extra sheen, body, and richness, and then a bit more mustard to taste. Transfer the brisket to a platter, spoon the thickened gravy over the meat, and serve.

Grandma's "secret" recipe . . .

Season a beef brisket heavily with salt and pepper, and transfer to roasting pan, fat-side up. Add a packet of Lipton onion soup mix, a can of Coca-Cola, a bottle of Heinz chili sauce (yes, the entire bottle), a few thinly sliced yellow onions, and some chopped carrots. Cook for 3 hours in a 350°F [180°C] oven.

Apricot Chicken

Serves 4 to 6

2 lb [910 g] bone-in, skin-on
chicken thighs or leg quarters

2 tsp Diamond Crystal kosher salt

Freshly ground black pepper

2 Tbsp vegetable oil

1 large yellow onion, thinly sliced

4 sprigs thyme

4 garlic cloves, peeled and smashed

¼ cup [45 g] chopped dried apricots

¼ cup plus 2 Tbsp [90 ml] apple cider vinegar

½ cup [120 ml] low-sodium chicken broth,
homemade stock (page 55), or water

2 Tbsp golden brown sugar

2 Tbsp soy sauce

No one ever seems to do this beloved dish justice. We were determined to change that. Ours benefits from a good hit of acid in the form of apple cider vinegar and a splash of umami: soy sauce. Searing the chicken first gives it a deeper flavor.

Preheat the oven to 375°F [190°C]. Using paper towels, pat the chicken dry. Place the chicken on a large platter and season both sides heavily with the salt and pepper.

Heat the oil in a large Dutch oven over medium-high heat until shimmering. Use tongs to lay the chicken, skin-side down, in the hot oil, working in batches if needed to prevent overcrowding and promote even browning. Sear, undisturbed, for 7 to 8 minutes, until well browned, and flip. Cook on the second side for 3 to 5 minutes more, until browned. Set aside the chicken on a large plate.

Turn the heat to medium and add the onion, thyme, and garlic to the pot. Toss with the fat from the chicken and sauté for 3 to 4 minutes, until the onion is translucent. Add the apricots and stir to combine. Cook for 1 minute. Add the vinegar to the pot and deglaze, using a wooden spoon to scrape up the browned bits from the bottom of the pot. Cook for 2 minutes more. Whisk in the stock, brown sugar, and soy sauce and cook for 1 minute more. Remove from the heat and return the seared chicken to the pot, tossing with the sauce and onions.

Arrange the chicken skin-side up and put the pot, uncovered, in the center of the oven. Cook for 12 to 15 minutes, until an instant-read thermometer inserted into the center of a thigh registers 165°F [75°C]. Transfer the chicken to a large rimmed platter or shallow bowl and pour the sauce and onions over the top to smother it. Leftover chicken will keep in an airtight container in the refrigerator for up to 5 days.

Carrot Tzimmes

Serves 8

2 Tbsp orange juice

1½ Tbsp golden brown sugar

1 Tbsp apple cider vinegar

2 Tbsp unsalted butter

2 lb [910 g] carrots, peeled, halved lengthwise, and cut crosswise into 1 in [2.5 cm] pieces

¼ cup [35 g] raisins

¼ cup [45 g] dried apricots, chopped

1 tsp Diamond Crystal kosher salt

¾ tsp ground cinnamon

⅛ tsp ground cardamom

1 dried bay leaf

1 star anise

3 Tbsp honey

Freshly ground black pepper

Chopped fresh tarragon
or parsley for garnish

Consider this dish the Jewish answer to candied yams. Every household makes tzimmes a little bit differently, but it generally consists of sweet carrots and dried fruit. Our version is a bit more refined, and a bit more balanced due to the acid from the apple cider vinegar and the tart orange juice. The warm spices add a nice complexity, which feels right at home next to a rich plate of brisket. This recipe is also delicious cold the next day.

In a small bowl, combine the orange juice, brown sugar, and vinegar and set aside.

Melt the butter in a heavy-bottomed skillet over medium heat. Add the carrots and stir to combine. Add the orange juice mixture, the raisins, apricots, salt, cinnamon, cardamom, bay leaf, and star anise, stirring again with a wooden spoon or rubber spatula to blend.

Reduce the heat to medium-low, cover the pan with a tight-fitting lid, and cook at a low simmer until the carrots are just tender, about 10 minutes.

Remove the lid, and raise the heat to high. Add the honey and stir to combine. Cook until the liquid is reduced by half and the carrots are well coated with the glaze, stirring occasionally, about 3 to 4 minutes more. Remove from the heat, discard the bay leaf and star anise, and serve immediately, garnished with freshly ground black pepper and chopped fresh herbs. Store in the refrigerator in a tightly sealed container for up to 5 days.

Potato Kugel

Serves 6 to 8

1 medium yellow onion, peeled and trimmed, with root end intact

1½ lb [680 g] skin-on russet potatoes, scrubbed

6 large eggs, lightly beaten

2 Tbsp vegetable oil

¼ cup [30 g] Streit's matzo meal

1 Tbsp Diamond Crystal kosher salt

2 tsp onion powder

¼ tsp freshly ground black pepper

Flaky sea salt for serving (optional)

Most of us don't have fond memories of kugel. Let's be honest: It can taste kind of boring. But not ours! It's crisp and pillowy.

Whenever we bake it at the deli, the aroma brings me back to my grandma's house in West LA, with her pink enamel twin ovens. Kugel is my madeleine. This kugel tastes even better when made 1 or 2 days in advance. Cut into portions and sear before serving.

Preheat the oven to 400°F [200°C]. Grate the onion on the large holes of a box grater into a medium bowl. You should have about 1 cup [230 g] of grated onion with liquid. Set aside.

Shred the potatoes on the large holes of the grater into another medium bowl, working quickly to prevent browning. Working in batches, use your bare hands or wrap the shredded potatoes in cheesecloth, and squeeze out the water over a bowl or sink; discard the water. Transfer the potatoes to the bowl with the onion and mix.

Set a medium well-seasoned cast-iron skillet over medium-low heat for about 5 minutes. Add enough oil or butter to lightly coat the pan, and spread it around with a paper towel.

While the pan is heating, add the eggs and 2 Tbsp of oil to the bowl with the potato-onion mixture, and mix well to combine. Add the matzo meal, kosher salt, onion powder, and pepper and mix again.

Add the kugel batter to the now-warm skillet and gently tamp down with the back of a spoon to even. The edges should start to slightly bubble and set in the preheated pan.

Place the skillet in the hot oven and bake for 40 to 45 minutes, until the tip of a knife or a cake tester inserted into the middle of the kugel comes out clean. The top of the kugel will be evenly browned.

Remove from the oven and let cool for about 10 minutes. Invert the kugel onto a plate, and serve.

The kugel can be cooled completely, wrapped well in plastic or aluminum foil, and refrigerated for up to 2 days. To serve, cut into equal pieces. Heat a cast-iron skillet over medium-high heat with about 1 Tbsp of vegetable oil or butter per serving. Sear the kugel pieces on both cut sides until golden brown. Serve with a pinch of flaky sea salt.

K for P Pineapple Upside-Down Cake

Makes one 10 in [25 cm] cake

2 Tbsp melted coconut oil

½ cup [100 g] packed dark brown sugar

One 20 oz [565 g] can sliced pineapple rings, drained

¼ cup plus 2 Tbsp [30 g] sifted matzo meal or matzo cake meal (preferably Streit's; use a fine-mesh strainer to sift)

3 Tbsp potato starch

⅛ tsp ground cardamom

1 Tbsp fresh orange juice

1½ tsp grated orange zest

1½ tsp fresh lemon juice

¾ tsp grated lemon zest

5 large eggs, separated, at room temperature

¼ tsp Diamond Crystal kosher salt

½ cup [100 g] granulated sugar

This is based on Safta Rickey's Passover sponge cake. Remember sponge cake? It was a big Bloom family hit and one of my safta's more memorable baked goods. Our cake is even better, as it combines her recipe with my personal favorite, pineapple upside-down cake.

Preheat the oven to 325°F [165°C]. Generously grease a 10 in [25 cm] springform pan with coconut oil or cooking spray. Line the bottom of the pan with a round of parchment paper, and grease the parchment as well.

In a small mixing bowl, mix together the coconut oil and brown sugar. With your hands or a rubber spatula, press the topping into an even layer on the bottom of the pan. (This may be a bit tricky since the pan and parchment are well greased and the sugar is coated in oil, but do your best to evenly distribute the mixture—it doesn't have to be perfect.) Place one pineapple ring in the center of the pan on top of the brown sugar mixture, and continue to fill the surface with pineapple rings in an even layer. Cut any of the remaining rings into quarters and arrange them in pieces along the outsides of the rings to fill in any gaps.

Put the sifted matzo meal in a small bowl. Add the potato starch and cardamom and whisk together until thoroughly combined and no visual lumps remain. Set aside. Mix the orange juice and zest and lemon juice and zest together in a small bowl and set aside.

In the bowl of a stand mixer fitted with a whisk attachment (or in a large bowl, using a handheld mixer), whip the egg whites at medium-high speed until frothy, about 1 minute. With the mixer still running, add the salt, and then increase the speed to high. Continue to whisk until soft peaks form, about 1 to 2 minutes. Turn down the mixer speed to medium and gradually add ¼ cup [50 g] of the sugar, a little at a time, increasing the speed to medium-high after each addition and then back down again to medium when adding more sugar. Stop the mixer and scrape down the sides of the bowl to ensure all of the sugar is incorporated into the egg whites. Continue to whip on high speed until stiff peaks form and the mixture is smooth and glossy, another minute or so. In total, the process of whipping the egg whites will take about 5 minutes.

Transfer the egg white mixture to a clean bowl, and quickly rinse the mixer bowl and dry with a paper towel. Add the egg yolks, and whisk at medium-high speed until combined, about 30 seconds. Turn down the mixer speed to medium and gradually add the remaining ¼ cup [50 g] of sugar. Stop and scrape down the sides and bottom of the bowl to incorporate any stray sugar. Increase the mixer speed to high and beat for about 3 minutes, until the egg yolks are pale and thick, and when the whisk is lifted out of the bowl, a trail of egg yolk falls slowly into the bowl in a ribbon.

Remove the bowl from the mixer. Add half the dry ingredients to the egg yolk mixture, and fold with a spatula to combine. Add half of the citrus juice and zest mixture and fold to combine, making sure to scrape the sides and bottom of the bowl throughout the folding process. Fold in the remaining dry ingredients and then the last of the citrus mixture. Mix in about a quarter of the white egg mixture to lighten the batter. Add the rest of the egg whites, and fold them in gently to combine without deflating. Scrape the sides and bottom of the bowl one last time to ensure everything is incorporated.

Pour the batter into the prepared pan, on top of the brown sugar mixture and pineapple rings, smoothing and leveling the surface. Bake for about 40 minutes, until the cake is set, nicely browned, and springs back to the touch. Cool the cake in the pan for 10 minutes. Run a knife between the cake and the sides of the pan, and release the sides of the springform pan. Being careful not to burn yourself, place a plate over the cake and invert the cake onto the plate. Remove the bottom of the pan, and peel off the parchment paper. Serve the cake warm.

To store the cake, cool completely. It will keep at room temperature, preferably under a domed lid, for up to 8 hours. (If you don't have a cake dome, try the bottom of a salad spinner.) After that, wrap tightly and refrigerate for up to 3 days.

True Complaints from the Kids' Table

"Every Passover and Hanukkah, and whenever we have a big Shabbat dinner, there's a kids' table. I'm seventeen, and I'm still sitting there. We've got all ages. My youngest cousin is six, we have an eight-year-old, a ten-year-old, my brother is fourteen. I'm basically the babysitter. It's messy, chaotic. We drink grape juice. Our settings are less done up, for sure. When they run out of regular glasses, we get plastic. Our place mats are usually the ones we've had since we were little: trucks or ballerinas. Even if it's just one big table, they still segregate us: kids at one end, adults at the other.

There are a lot of strong personalities at the kids' table. It's like a giant competition. Everyone is always fighting over whose school is better and comparing grades. My brother and cousin like to argue over politics. I'm, like, if we're going to talk politics, we might as well be at the adults' table. When it gets too intense, I just get up and move over. It's calmer there. They never send me back, but I wonder when they'll actually invite me to sit with them? Maybe when I'm eighteen? Twenty-one?

For now, I guess I'll just appreciate the upside: We always get served first."

—**Mia, Berkeley**

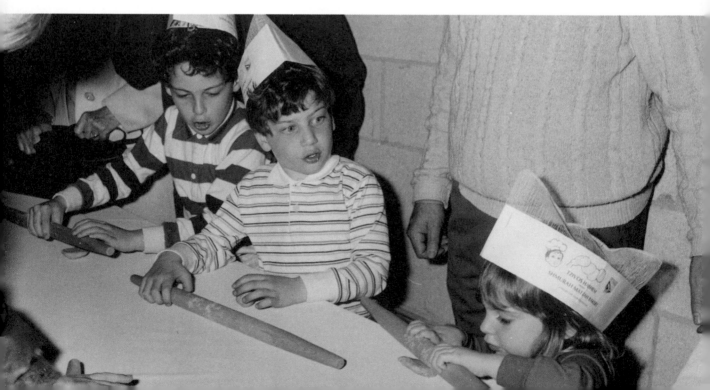

In Praise of Parsley

Always a garnish, never a star. Except on this night. Passover is parsley's night to shine! And every year, as we dip our leafy, featherlight stalks in saltwater, I make a silent promise to myself to eat more of it all year long. And people are. "It's on its way to becoming the new kale," legendary seed farmer Frank Morton once told me. He experiments with parsley samples from around the world—Hungary, Poland, Iran—in an effort to breed all sorts of hardy, flavorful varieties. But the bright, robust, slightly bitter taste of good old flat-leaf Italian is just fine. Old tip, from Grandpa Sam, a dentist: Chewing a sprig is the next best thing to brushing.

On the Afikomen

The Too-Obvious Hiding Places
- Under the throw pillow or blanket on the couch
- Behind the family photos on the fireplace mantle
- In the top drawer of the table in the front hall
- Between two books on the bookshelf

"My papa always tucked the afikomen into the pillowcase of the pillow he rested on throughout the Seder," recalls one former child. "If we wanted it, we had to be wily—grab it when he got up or wasn't paying attention."

—Deanne, San Francisco

 Parents: If you want to buy some relaxing kid-free time at the table, don't make it too easy and let them run around for a while. Other suggested no-fail hiding places: in the refrigerator or under the welcome mat, outside, with Elijah.

Winner of the Hunt for the Afikomen

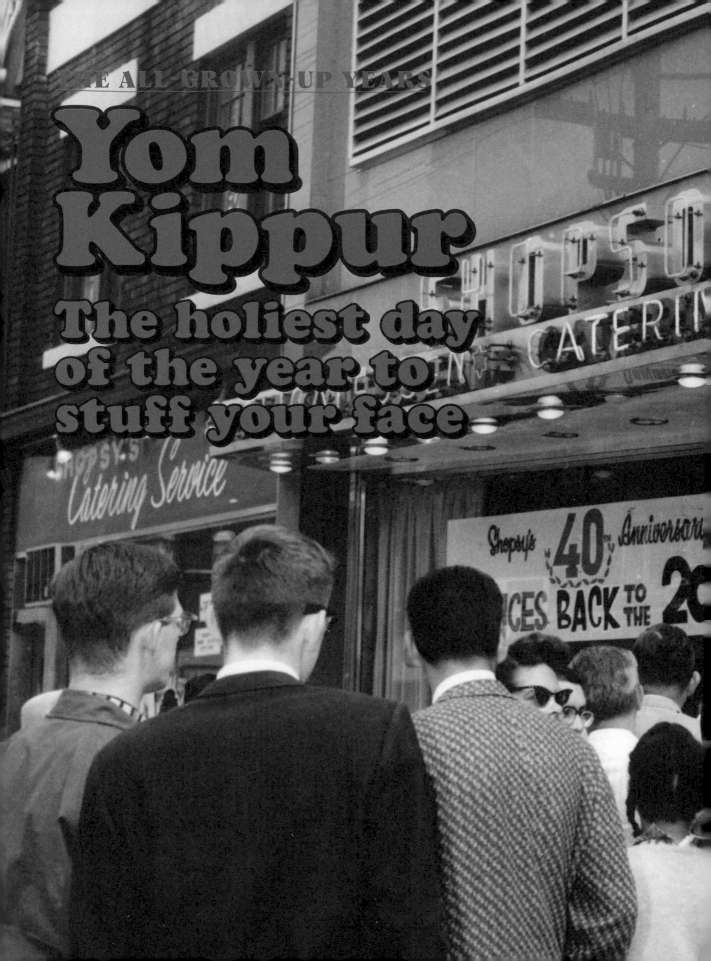

Yom Kippur

The holiest day of the year to stuff your face

Fasting Is Trending

Humans have been voluntarily withholding food in the name of spiritual and physical well-being for thousands of years, from Pythagoras to Benjamin Franklin to Beyoncé. But lately, it seems, everyone—friends, officemates, fathers—is fasting. Intermittent fasting. Water fasting. Juice fasting. Master cleanse–fasting. Fanatically fasting all the freaking time.

It sounds far more noble, and a little less annoying, when people fast for religious reasons, though, doesn't it?

Buddhists do it. Muslims do it. Baha'is do it. Catholics do it. And, even though the Talmud actually urges us to take advantage of every opportunity to eat, Jews—reluctantly, and not without whining, and certainly not all of us—do it, too.

Why, though? Because we are also told, by the Torah, that we must reflect and repent—and afflict our souls on Yom Kippur, the holiest day of the Jewish year. And, really, what better way for Jews to torment themselves than by not eating for an entire twenty-five hours? (Yes, twenty-five hours, not twenty-four. Apparently sundown-to-sundown is a little too loosey-goosey, so we're supposed to tack on an extra hour, just to be safe.)

After all these years, after so much suffering, fasting should really be easier than the ladies of *Broad City* make it sound:

> *"We've got four hours until the sunset,"* Abbi *says to* Ilana, *via Skype, as they lie, famished, on their respective beds.*
>
> *"I know we're not supposed to be this hungry,"* says Abbi.
>
> *"We are monsters!"* replies Ilana.

And soon enough, they both cave and tear into bacon-egg-and-cheese sandwiches.

> *"I don't feel bad!"* says Ilana. *"This is living!"*

She's got a point. As the old Jewish joke goes—inevitably told by some middle-aged man named Joel digging into a lobster—"Don't you think the Jews have suffered enough?"

No matter why you fast, or how you fast, eventually you have to break the fast. There are all sorts of slow, civilized strategies for "easing out" or "reintroducing," as the Goopies say. But slow and civilized is not the Jewish way.

To break the fast, Yom Kippur style, is to come straight from temple wearing loose clothing, perhaps an elastic waistband, and barge into your best Jewish friends' house, barely say hello, and storm the buffet table.

However, there is another set of break the fasters: those who know to hang back and let those who are actually hungry eat first.

It is a widely held belief that break the fasts are not just for fasters alone.

Sure, you might feel better about cramming your plate with bagels and cream cheese and lox and kugel and egg salad and chicken salad and whitefish salad if you *do* fast. But as every cultural Jew knows: No one will think any less of you if you don't.

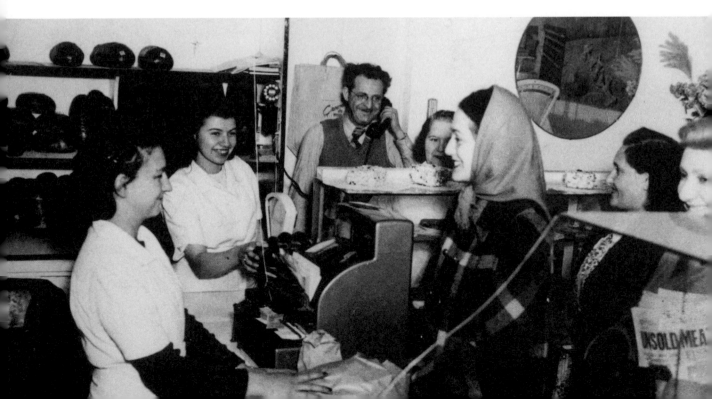

Deli Salads

Chicken Salad

Makes 3 cups [740 g]

12 oz [340 g] shredded or roughly chopped cooked chicken (page 55)

¾ cup [180 g] mayonnaise

3 Tbsp whole-grain Dijon or brown deli mustard

½ cup [75 g] finely chopped red onion

½ cup [60 g] finely chopped celery

3 Tbsp finely chopped fresh parsley

2 Tbsp finely chopped fresh dill

1 Tbsp fresh lemon juice

2 tsp onion powder

2 tsp garlic powder

1 tsp Diamond Crystal kosher salt

1 tsp finely ground black pepper

A deli staple, ours has a bit of a "ranch"-style flavor from the onion and garlic powders and loads of fresh herbs. We serve it as a sandwich on toasted challah with lettuce and tomato.

In a medium bowl, combine the chicken, mayonnaise, mustard, onion, celery, herbs, lemon juice, onion powder, garlic powder, salt, and pepper and stir to combine. (We like to mix this until the chicken breaks up into smaller pieces.) Let the mixture rest for 15 minutes to allow the flavors to marry. The chicken salad will keep in an airtight container in the refrigerator for up to 3 days.

Smoked Fish Salad

Makes 2 cups [650 g]

1 lb [455 g] boneless hot-smoked fish, such as whitefish or trout, flaked or ground

½ cup [120 g] whole milk Greek yogurt or mayonnaise

¼ cup [30 g] finely chopped celery

2 Tbsp fresh lemon juice

2 tsp chopped fresh dill

2 tsp chopped fresh parsley

Freshly ground black pepper

We like smoked whitefish or trout, but hot-smoked salmon would work well, too. Most smoked fish is already pretty salty, so we omit salt from this recipe. Fresh herbs lend vibrancy, and the Greek yogurt, while optional, makes for a lighter salad than the traditional mayonnaise.

In a large mixing bowl, break up the smoked fish with your hands so there are no large clumps, and it will be easier to mix. Add the yogurt, celery, lemon juice, dill, parsley, and pepper and fold together with a rubber spatula until well combined.

The fish salad will keep in an airtight container in the refrigerator for up to 1 week.

Tuna Salad

Makes 2 cups [265 g]

One 5 oz [142 g] can water-packed albacore tuna, drained

5 Tbsp [75 g] mayonnaise

1 Tbsp whole-grain Dijon
or brown deli mustard

2 Tbsp finely chopped red onion

2 Tbsp finely chopped celery

2 Tbsp finely chopped fresh dill

1 tsp fresh lemon juice, plus ¼ tsp grated
lemon zest, and lemon wedges for serving

A perfect tuna melt is served on toasted Jewish rye with melted Cheddar, some fresh greens, and our Pickled Mustard Seeds (see page 215).

¾ tsp Diamond Crystal kosher salt

½ tsp freshly ground black pepper

In a medium bowl, fold together the tuna, mayonnaise, mustard, onion, celery, dill, lemon juice, and zest. Season with salt and pepper and serve with lemon wedges.

The tuna salad will keep in an airtight container in the refrigerator for up to 3 days.

Egg Salad

Makes 2½ cups [585 g]

6 large eggs

¼ cup plus 1 Tbsp [75 g] mayonnaise

2 Tbsp whole-grain Dijon or brown deli mustard

3 Tbsp finely chopped red onion

3 Tbsp finely chopped celery

1 Tbsp finely chopped fresh dill,
plus extra for garnish

1 Tbsp finely chopped fresh parsley

1 tsp sweet paprika

Diamond Crystal kosher salt

Freshly ground black pepper

Bread and butter pickles, for garnish

When we created our egg salad, we wanted it to be as straightforward as possible. It's all about consistency and the ratio of eggs to mayo—and of course, the accoutrements. We serve it open-faced on toasted bread with arugula, a little fresh dill, pepper, and the clincher: bread and butter pickles.

Bring a medium pot of water to a gentle boil over medium-high heat. Use a slotted spoon to carefully lower the eggs into the water, one by one. Adjust the heat to maintain a gentle boil and cook the eggs for 10 minutes. Meanwhile, fill a large pot, bowl, or container with ice and half as much water. Remove the eggs from the pot and plunge them into the ice water bath for about 5 minutes. Peel the eggs once they've cooled.

Transfer the eggs to a medium bowl, and use the back of a fork to break them up into small chunks, about the size of peas. Add the mayonnaise, mustard, onion, celery, dill, parsley, and paprika. Season with salt and pepper. Mix well with a wooden spoon to combine, gently folding the ingredients, without smashing the eggs. Garnish with more dill and the bread and butter pickles. The egg salad will keep in an airtight container in the refrigerator for up to 3 days.

Potato Salad

Makes 7 cups [1.6 kg]

3 lb [1.4 kg] skin-on Yukon gold potatoes, cut into ½ in [12 mm] cubes

1 cup [240 g] mayonnaise

2½ Tbsp whole-grain Dijon mustard

2 Tbsp white wine vinegar

2 Tbsp minced nonpareil capers

1 Tbsp finely chopped fresh dill

1 Tbsp finely chopped fresh parsley

2 tsp white sugar

¼ cup [40 g] finely chopped red onion

¼ cup [30 g] finely chopped celery

1 Tbsp Diamond Crystal kosher salt

I could eat this potato salad with every meal, including breakfast—and when we first started Wise Sons, Leo and I did. Yukon gold potatoes provide creaminess, capers pack a salty punch, and heaps of fresh herbs keep it bright.

Bring a large pot of salted water to a boil. Add the potatoes, lower the heat, and simmer the potatoes for about 15 minutes, until very tender. Drain in a colander and spread out on a baking sheet to cool.

In a medium bowl combine the mayonnaise, mustard, vinegar, capers, dill, parsley, and sugar. Whisk together until well combined.

Combine the cooled potatoes, onion, celery, and salt in a large bowl. Slowly add the dressing, and fold to combine, using a large spoon. The mixture should be creamy, with some chunks of potatoes. Refrigerate for at least 1 hour before serving. The potato salad will keep in an airtight container in the refrigerator for up to 5 days.

Coleslaw

Makes 4 cups [480 g]

½ cup [120 g] mayonnaise

1 Tbsp plus 1 tsp extra-hot prepared horseradish

1 Tbsp sugar

1 Tbsp puréed yellow onion

2 tsp cold water

1 tsp fresh lemon juice

½ tsp whole-grain or coarse Dijon mustard

¼ tsp celery seeds

½ tsp Diamond Crystal kosher salt

½ tsp freshly ground black pepper

4 cups [270 g] shredded green cabbage

½ cup [35 g] shredded red cabbage

¼ cup [30 g] shredded carrots

This is the coleslaw we serve at our deli. Classically sweet, with celery seeds and an unexpected kick from horseradish and puréed onions, it's especially good inside a sandwich, like Langer's famous #19 pastrami sandwich (the best sandwich in the world). In homage, we include it on our menu: untoasted rye, a shmear of Russian dressing, two slices of cold Swiss, hot pastrami, and, in between, a fat pile of slaw.

In a large bowl, whisk together the mayonnaise, horseradish, sugar, onion, water, lemon juice, and mustard until smooth. Stir in the celery seeds, salt, and pepper. Add the cabbages and the carrots to the bowl and toss well to combine. Refrigerate until cold.

We prefer to eat this within a few hours of preparation, but it will keep, covered, in the refrigerator for 1 day.

Wedding Party
The day every Jewish mother dreams of

Premarital Misery

A brief recap of my Jewish wedding, which could very well be any Jewish wedding:

My mother got shingles in the weeks leading up to it, due to stress. The guest list ballooned to over 200 because of the 92 people she *had* to invite. The venue we chose was "too rustic." She hated the idea of using mason jars in lieu of "real vases" for flowers. And we weren't allowed to have pie. It's not that she preferred we have a traditional tiered cake. (She didn't, we didn't.) It's just that pie, my mother said, wasn't "appropriate." At least she didn't have to contend with Evan's menu for his wedding: a whole nose-to-hoof pig, slow-roasted, on display, ultimately picked clean. (Albeit eaten on homemade challah buns.)

Meanwhile, our ceremony couldn't start until after sundown, because there wasn't a rabbi in all of Northern California who'd do it before the end of Shabbat. So by the time the alfresco dinner was served, everyone was freezing. One uncle had a minor diabetic attack. Another passed out because he'd smuggled in a joint and took too big a hit. In the melee that was making seating charts, I'd accidentally seated two warring sides of my husband's family together, despite their specific requests they be seated far, far apart. And, at the end of what really was a magical weekend, my eighty-nine-year-old grandmother, who'd flown in from Florida, declared she'd done so for only one reason: "Otherwise, I wouldn't be in the photos—and everyone would think I was dead."

Weddings are stressful for everyone, but for some reason, they seem to be most stressful for Jewish parents of a certain generation. "I think in Jewish families, we tend to be much more up in each other's business," says Jewish wedding expert Karen Cinnamon, founder of the blog *Smashing the Glass*. "One bride's parents told her outright, 'This is our wedding. When your daughter gets married, that will be your wedding.'"

And yet, despite all the drama and debates, the Jewish wedding is itself a wonderful thing. Its two-thousand-year-old traditions are so simple, so timeless. (The whole dowry-mohar-possession parts notwithstanding.) We drink from a single cup of wine to signify our shared life! We circle each other a dizzying seven times to signify our protection of one another! It's sweet. It makes sense. Some customs are so compelling, they transcend the realm of religion and are being more widely embraced. Italians are stomping on glass to cries of "Mazel Tov!" from the crowd. Episcopalians are signing ketubahs (marriage contracts). And betrothed couples of all backgrounds are getting hitched under a chuppah. "It's a message with pretty universal appeal," says Cinnamon. "Now that engaged couples have so much more exposure to wedding traditions outside their own, through the internet and social media, it's no surprise, the chuppah is catching on."

And they've become quite fashionable, going beyond the classic white linen look to include everything from Lucite to vintage lace, copper to rose gold, pretty origami paper cranes to preppy Pendelton blankets. Some might call it a canopy. Regardless, propped up by family or friends, it symbolizes the same thing: the home—and the life—that you and your beloved will build together.

But, the most modern-day Jewish wedding tradition remains that existential, often unsatisfying choice. One that must be marked, a month in advance, on the RSVP card: Beef, Chicken, or Fish?

Always-Perfect Oven-Poached Salmon

Serves 4

¼ cup [60 g] mayonnaise

1 Tbsp plus 1 tsp kosher salt

Four 6 oz [170 g] skin-on salmon fillets, about 2 in [5 cm] wide, patted dry with a paper towel

1 bunch fresh dill, separated into 4 smaller bunches, plus 1 Tbsp roughly chopped

16 lemon wheels, about ⅛ in [4 mm] thick (from about 2 lemons), plus 1 lemon, cut into wedges

My mom was born and raised in Vancouver, Canada, where salmon is, er, king. We ate salmon like Americans eat chicken: all the time. She'd cook a whole side of fish, using this method. It's a recipe that works well in the oven or on the grill, and it's great for a crowd if you can stomach the price. Although farmed salmon is actually best here, as it's nice and fatty.

Preheat the oven to 350°F [180°C].

In a medium bowl, whisk together the mayonnaise and salt. Lay out a sheet of heavy-duty aluminum foil roughly 12 in [30.5 cm] square on a flat surface and place one salmon fillet in the center, skin-side down. Slather 1 Tbsp of the mayonnaise mixture all over the salmon, including the skin, coating the fish evenly. Return the salmon to the center of the foil. Lay a small bunch of dill sprigs on top of the salmon, and arrange 4 lemon wheels across the top in a line. Carefully fold up the edges of the foil to make a packet, and crimp the seams. (This will help keep the steam inside and keep the fish moist when cooking.) Repeat the process with the remaining salmon fillets. At this point the packets are ready to cook, but they can be stored in the refrigerator overnight.

Space the four salmon packets evenly on a large rimmed baking sheet. Bake for 20 minutes and remove from the oven. Immediately open each packet, being careful not to burn your fingers as the hot steam escapes. The salmon will easily pull away from the skin, if desired, or it can be carefully removed whole with a flat spatula.

The salmon can be served hot right away, at room temperature, or cold. Sprinkle with chopped fresh dill and serve with lemon wedges. Leftover salmon will keep in a tightly sealed container in the refrigerator for up to 5 days.

Cooked salmon is extremely versatile. It's great scrambled with eggs and onions; stuffed into a toasted sandwich with a slice of tomato and crisp lettuce; shredded over salad greens; or in a creamy fish salad. My favorite is to blend 1 part chopped smoked salmon, 1 part poached salmon, and 2 parts sour cream; it makes a great party dip.

Chicken Schnitzel

Serves 4 to 6

Four 8 oz [225 g] boneless, skinless air-chilled chicken breasts

Diamond Crystal kosher salt

2 cups [280 g] all-purpose flour

6 large eggs, beaten

4 cups [240 g] panko

6 Tbsp [60 g] sesame seeds

Vegetable oil for frying

1 cup [250 g] Lemon-Caper Mayonnaise (recipe follows) for serving

Salad greens for serving

Pat the chicken dry with paper towels. Use a sharp chef's knife to butterfly each breast: Place your hand on the top of the breast and use the other hand to run the knife through the breast horizontally, cutting almost through to the other side. Place one chicken breast in a 1 gal [3.8 L] resealable plastic bag or between two sheets of plastic wrap on a cutting board. Use a small saucepan or meat mallet to pound the breast flat and even, working from the center out toward the edges, until the breast is about ⅛ in [4 mm] thick. Repeat with the remaining chicken breasts. Season the breasts on each side with salt and set aside to dry brine for 15 minutes.

Meanwhile, set up three rimmed plates or wide, shallow bowls for your dredging station: Put the flour in one bowl, the eggs in the second, and the panko crumbs in the third. Mix the sesame seeds with the panko crumbs. Using one hand for wet ingredients and one for dry, dip the chicken in the flour, shaking off any excess, then dip it in the egg, coating both sides. Place the chicken in the panko and turn to carefully coat. Set aside on a plate and repeat with the remaining chicken.

Jews don't own schnitzel, but we eat it like we do. Crisp and golden on the outside, juicy and tender on the inside. This was one of the most popular specials we've ever run at Wise Sons. We set the schnitzel between two thick-cut, griddled slices of challah, then slathered it with the mayo, arugula, and pickled onions—and promptly sold out.

Line a baking sheet with paper towels. Pour enough oil into a large cast-iron skillet or Dutch oven to reach a depth of ½ in [12 mm]. Heat over medium-high heat for 5 minutes, until shimmering. Carefully place one piece of chicken in the middle of the skillet and cook for 4 to 5 minutes until golden brown around the edges. Use tongs or a fork to flip the chicken and cook the other side for 3 to 4 minutes more until golden brown all over. Transfer to the prepared baking sheet. Repeat with the remaining chicken.

Season the cooked chicken with more salt and serve with the Lemon-Caper Mayonnaise and salad greens. Leftover chicken will keep in a resealable plastic bag in the refrigerator for up to 5 days. Makes a great cold chicken sandwich!

Lemon-Caper Mayonnaise

1 cup [240 g] mayonnaise

2 Tbsp fresh lemon juice, plus 1 tsp grated lemon zest

1 Tbsp plus 1 tsp nonpareil capers, drained and chopped

½ tsp whole-grain Dijon mustard

Freshly ground black pepper

In a small bowl, stir together the mayonnaise, lemon juice and zest, capers, and mustard, and season with pepper. The mayonnaise will keep in an airtight container in the refrigerator for up to 1 week. Makes about 1 cup [250 g].

Roumanian Skirt Steak

Serves 4

One 1 lb [455 g] skirt or hanger steak, about 2 in [5 cm] thick, cut into 4 pieces

4 tsp sweet paprika

4 tsp Diamond Crystal kosher salt

3 Tbsp vegetable oil or other neutral oil

1 bunch scallions, root ends trimmed

Scallion Sauce (recipe follows)

Freshly ground black pepper

Silver Dollar Potatoes (page 194) for serving (optional)

This garlicky skirt steak, marinated in lots of garlic and sometimes paprika, hails from the mother country. It's a whole flank steak. In the United States, this dish is synonymous with Sammy's Romanian on the Lower East Side of New York, served with tableside chopped liver, dill pickles, roasted green peppers, and a bottle of vodka encased in ice.

This is our version, with a chimichurri-like sauce. We add grilled whole scallions, because grilled whole scallions are great on pretty much anything—but especially on this.

Set the steaks out on a plate or cutting board. If damp, pat dry with paper towels. Combine the paprika and salt in a small bowl, and season the steaks on both sides with the mixture. Let rest, uncovered, for about 30 minutes at room temperature.

Heat a large well-seasoned cast-iron skillet over high heat until smoking hot. Add 1 Tbsp of the oil and the whole scallions. Sear until evenly caramelized, about 6 to 8 minutes, turning them occasionally with tongs. The root end may not cook as fast as the stalks, and that is OK. There will be a nice balance between the charred green stems and the more piquant white bulbs. Transfer to a plate and set aside.

Wipe the skillet clean with a damp paper towel and let the skillet rest with the heat still on high for about 2 minutes, until it is smoking again. Add 1 Tbsp of oil and swirl around to coat the entire bottom of the skillet.

Turn the heat to medium-high and place two of the steaks in the hot skillet, being careful not to crowd the pan, as you want a nice crust to form. For a medium steak, cook for 3 minutes, without disturbing, and then flip the steak and cook for 1 minute more on the second side. Remove the steak from the skillet and let it rest on a plate or cutting board for at least

5 minutes. Repeat with the remaining 1 Tbsp of oil and the remaining two steaks. Cut the steaks on an angle, against the grain, into ¼ in [6 mm] thick slices.

Top each steak with a spoonful of garlic sauce, a few charred scallions, and few grinds of pepper. Serve the potatoes alongside, if you wish.

Scallion Sauce

1 bunch fresh parsley, thick stems trimmed

¾ cup [100 g] garlic cloves, peeled and trimmed

1 cup [48 g] thinly sliced scallions (green and white parts, about 5 scallions)

½ tsp Diamond Crystal kosher salt

1¼ cups [300 ml] good-quality olive oil

Grated zest and juice of 1 large lemon (about ¼ cup [60 ml] juice)

In the bowl of a food processor, combine the parsley and garlic and pulse until they form a coarse paste. Do not overprocess. Transfer to a medium bowl, and add the scallions, salt, oil, and lemon zest and juice. Stir well to combine. Set aside for at least 1 hour to let the flavors marry. (The sauce will keep, covered, in the refrigerator for up to 1 week.) Makes about 2½ cups [360 ml].

Silver Dollar Potatoes

Serves 4

Diamond Crystal kosher salt

2 lb [910 g] skin-on large Yukon gold potatoes, sliced into ¼ in [6 mm] thick rounds

2 Tbsp olive oil

In a large pot, bring 8 cups [2 L] of water to a rolling boil over high heat and season with 2 Tbsp salt. Lower the heat to medium-high and place the potato rounds in the boiling water. Cook for 7 to 9 minutes, until just tender. Carefully remove the potatoes with a wire mesh skimmer or slotted spoon and transfer to a baking sheet or platter to cool. Discard the water. Draining the potatoes in a colander may break them into pieces. (At this

These sop up all the juices. Save some for breakfast: It's to die faw, with a fried egg on top.

point, the potatoes can be stored, covered, in the refrigerator overnight.)

Transfer the potatoes to a large bowl, add the oil and 1½ tsp salt, and use your hands to carefully toss the potatoes to coat. Remove from the bowl and lay out the potatoes on a clean baking sheet in a single layer, leaving space between them where possible to encourage browning, rather than steaming.

Roast for 20 minutes, until the bottom side is evenly browned. Flip each potato round so they brown on both sides. Return the potatoes to the oven and roast for 5 minutes more. Serve immediately.

. . . And the Passed Apps

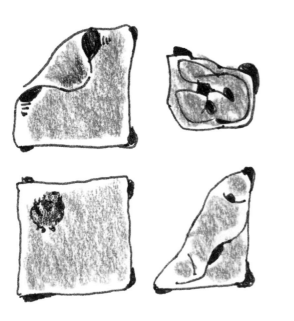

Gyoza Kreplach

Makes about 45 kreplach

Jewish dumplings! Kreplach are quite a delicious, heimish bite. While Bubbe might have made her dough from scratch, not everyone has the time, or forearms, for that. The secret is a premade wonton wrapper. Many supermarkets carry them.

Start with about **1 lb [455 g] or so of leftover brisket** (page 167), patted dry. Throw it in the food processor with about **½ an onion** that you've already caramelized, **an egg**, and **salt and pepper** (or chop everything reeeeally well). Many culinary traditions have a "holy trinity," which is the basis of its cuisine, such as a soffrito (Italian) or a mirepoix (Cajun and Creole). Jewish food has . . . onions. Pulse it all into a coarse paste, and transfer to a bowl.

Lay out a few "**kreplach wraps**" on a work surface and plop a few tsp of filling in the middle. Brush the edges of the wraps with a little water, and then fold each wrap over the filling to make a triangle. Press the edges together to seal. Now, take the two corners of your half-moon dumpling, bring them together, and pinch with a little more water. They look sort of like tortellini.

Fish Roe on a Mini Latke

Affordable and sophisticated! Fish roe never fails to impress. The tiny orange pearls of trout or salmon eggs are available at most grocery stores. Pair with Bagel Chips (page 199) or latkes (page 33).

Buy a tube of **sour cream** (it's a thing now), or dump your standard 1 lb [455 g] container into a resealable plastic bag, and snip the corner. Squeeze a dot of sour cream onto each **bagel chip or mini latke**, and add a couple of spoonfuls of **roe**. Garnish with **fresh dill**.

Cook in salted boiling water for 3 to 4 minutes (or according to the package directions) until they float. Drain the kreplach. In a nonstick or cast-iron pan, heat a healthy slick of **oil or schmaltz** over medium heat. Working in batches, crisp the kreplach on both sides. Serve with **sour cream** and some **fresh herbs**.

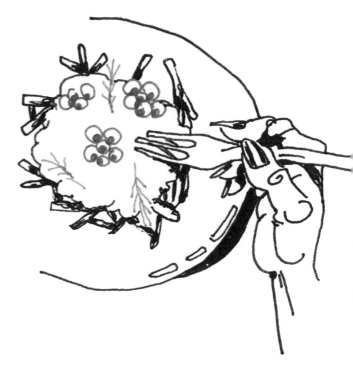

Chopped Liver Toast

This may not be as trendy as its avocado counterpart, but it's even tastier. We love chopped liver, though not necessarily for its looks. The classic deli scoop on a lettuce cup doesn't cut it. We like to gussy up our liver with a good sliced rye (although any bread will do).

Cut off the crusts and cut the **bread** into small rectangles. (Use the scraps for bread crumbs

or something.) Toss with a bit of **olive oil** and a few **pinches of salt**, then toast on a baking sheet at 350°F [180°C] for up to 20 minutes, flipping once or twice. Set aside to cool.

Now, grab a trusty soup spoon for the real artistry. Using the back of the spoon, gently swoosh enough **Chopped Liver** (page 165) to cover each toast from edge to edge in an even layer. Go easy so as not to overwhelm these delicate bites. Garnish with **finely chopped pickled onion** (page 215), **chopped fresh parsley leaves**, and a **grated hard-boiled egg** if you really want to go the extra mile.

Dinner with the Goyim In-Laws

What to cook? You're not going to serve them chopped liver! Or are you?

So, You Didn't Marry a Jew*

It happens, interfaith marriage. More and more. More on the West Coast than on the East Coast—and, word is, more among Jews than among other minority groups. In 2015, Pew's Religious Landscape Study found that more than three-quarters of Hindus (91 percent), Mormons (82 percent), and Muslims (79 percent) in the United States marry or move in with "the right kind," as Evan's safta put it (see page 106, "Are You Meeting New People?"). For Jews, it drops to 65 percent. And for Jews who married in 2005 or later, it's even lower: 58 percent.

Which means, in our global, increasingly intercultural world, all of these Jewish parents praying their daughter marries a mensch from Manhattan better prepare for the possibility that she shacks up, sans ring, with a nice Catholic woman from Mexico instead.

Jewish-Catholic is actually quite a popular combo. It even comes with a cute nickname ("Cashew"). Jewish-Protestant couples are common, too. (Should we call them JASPs?) According to a study of intermarried Jews, 39 percent were married to Catholics; 23 percent to Protestants.

The first time Evan went to dinner at his father-in-law's house in Sacramento, it was Christmas. They simmered mackerel and made mung-bean pancakes and, so sweet, set out a fork, among all the chopsticks, just for him. He's never cooked Jewish food for his Korean in-laws. Though they have come into the deli before, with eighty-five-year-old Halmeoni in tow. She fell in love with the cinnamon babka, and his mother-in-law admitted she liked Wise Sons' pastrami even better than her old favorite pastrami: Arby's.

All of which begs the question: What should you cook for your new non-Jewish in-laws?

The goal is to make the goyim feel comfortable. You know, the opposite of how Alvy Singer felt at Easter dinner at Annie Hall's house. For Jews who marry Koreans or Italians or Chinese or Indians or Greeks, it's not that hard. After all, all descendants of immigrants are used to sitting down to obscene amounts of food with family-style platters and people talking at decibel levels typically reserved for SoulCycle instructors.

Herewith, a menu fit for both the Finklesteins and the Fortenbaughs.

* *You did marry a Jew? Mazel.*
Double the recipes.

Everything Onion Dip

Serves 6 to 8

2 Tbsp vegetable oil

1 medium yellow onion, finely diced

Diamond Crystal kosher salt

1 cup [240 g] sour cream

¾ cup [180 g] cream cheese, at room temperature

2 Tbsp Everything Spice (page 92)

1 Tbsp onion powder

1 Tbsp Worcestershire sauce

1 Tbsp chopped fresh dill

1 Tbsp chopped fresh parsley

1 tsp sliced fresh chives or scallions

Never throw away your stale bagels again! Bagel chips come together as quickly as you'll eat them, and you'll want to eat them with this dip.

If you're like us, you grew up eating dip made with Lipton's French onion soup mix. This is our from-scratch take on that creamy umami bomb, with deeply caramelized onions.

Heat the olive oil in a large heavy-bottomed skillet over medium heat. Add the onion and sweat for 5 minutes. Add ⅛ tsp salt and turn the heat to medium-low. Cook for 35 to 45 minutes, stirring occasionally to prevent sticking, until the onion is soft and a deep golden brown. The onion should be almost jammy in consistency, with all of the sugars caramelized, making them sweet like candy. You should end up with about ½ cup [140 g] of cooked onion.

In a stand mixer fitted with a paddle attachment, whip the sour cream and cream cheese together on medium speed for about 1 minute. Add the onion mixture and mix for 1 minute more. Use a rubber spatula to scrape the mixture from the sides and bottom of the bowl. Add 1 Tbsp of the Everything Spice, the onion powder, Worcestershire, and 1 tsp salt and mix for about 1 minute more. Transfer to a container with a lid and refrigerate until firm, about 1 hour.

When ready to serve, spoon the dip into a wide bowl. Garnish with the remaining 1 Tbsp of Everything Spice, sprinkling it evenly over the surface. Top with the dill, parsley, and chives for that extra pizzazz. Serve with bagel chips or crudités. The dip will keep in an airtight container in the refrigerator for up to 5 days.

Bagel Chips

3 bagels (any flavor; a mix is best)

2 Tbsp vegetable oil

1 tsp Diamond Crystal kosher salt

½ tsp garlic powder

Preheat the oven to 350°F [180°C]. Slice the bagels about ⅛ in [4 mm] thick, and put in a large bowl. Add the oil, salt, and garlic powder and toss to combine.

Lightly oil a baking sheet with about 1 Tbsp of oil. Spread out the bagel slices evenly in one layer on the baking sheet. Bake the bagel slices in the oven for about 10 minutes, use a spatula to toss, and continue baking for 4 or 5 minutes more, until lightly browned.

Remove from the oven and let cool on the baking sheet. The bagel chips will keep in a resealable plastic bag or an airtight container at room temperature for up to 1 week. Serves 6 to 8.

Green Bean Casserole

Serves 6 to 8 (as a side)

1½ lb [680 g] mixed fresh green beans, such as Blue Lake, or yellow wax beans

3 Tbsp Schmaltz (page 56)

2 cups [280 g] diced yellow onion

12 oz [340 g] diced fresh mushrooms, such as a mix of shiitake, cremini, and beech

3 garlic cloves, minced

2 sprigs thyme

1 Tbsp brandy

1 cup [240 ml] homemade chicken stock (page 55) or low-sodium broth

½ cup [120 ml] heavy cream

2 Tbsp cornstarch

1 Tbsp Diamond Crystal kosher salt

¼ tsp freshly ground black pepper

½ cup [30 g] store-bought french-fried onions, plus more for garnish

2 Tbsp grated Parmesan cheese

2 Tbsp crispy chicken skin, left over from making schmaltz, lightly crushed

Dill sprigs for garnish

Dinners at non-Jewish friends' houses always seemed to include a version of this casserole, made with cream of mushroom soup and served with a glass of milk. Start with the best, freshest beans you can find for a superlative finished dish. If you can, freeze locally grown beans in the peak of summer to use in the winter, when this casserole is especially satisfying. The recipe is bulletproof.

Preheat the oven to 350°F [180°C]. Grease a 9 by 9 in [23 by 23 cm] casserole dish. Bring a large pot of heavily salted water to a boil.

While the water comes to a boil, trim the stems from the beans and cut them into bite-size pieces. When the water is at a rolling boil, add the beans and lower the heat to bring the water to a simmer. Cook for 5 minutes, drain the beans in a colander, and rinse with cold running water to stop the cooking process. Set aside.

In a large heavy-bottomed sauté pan over medium heat, melt the schmaltz. Add the onion and sauté until they are translucent. Add half of the mushrooms, the garlic, and the thyme. Continue to sauté until the mushrooms have cooked down to half their original size, stirring occasionally, 6 to 8 minutes. Add the rest of the mushrooms to the pan and stir to combine. Continue cooking until the mushrooms are tender and the onions are a light caramel color, about 8 minutes more. Increase the heat to high and splash in the brandy. Cook, stirring constantly, for about 30 seconds, then remove the pan from the heat.

In a small bowl, whisk together the chicken stock, heavy cream, and cornstarch until the cornstarch is completely dissolved. Add the mixture to the mushrooms and stir to combine. Turn the heat to medium-high and cook, stirring, until the sauce is as thick as mayonnaise. Fish out the thyme sprigs, and season with the salt and pepper.

Mix the fried onions and all of the blanched beans into the mushroom mixture. Or, if the pan isn't large enough, combine them in a large bowl. Pour the mixture into the prepared casserole dish. Garnish with more fried onions, the Parmesan, and chicken skins. Bake until bubbly, toasty, and golden, about 25 minutes. Serve immediately, garnished with fresh dill. The casserole will keep, covered, in the refrigerator for up to 5 days. Reheat at 350°F [180°C] for about 12 to 15 minutes.

Intermarriage Meat Loaf with Melted Onions

Serves 6 to 8

MEAT LOAF

3 slices stale challah,
homemade (page 125) or store bought

2 Tbsp Schmaltz (page 56)

1 cup [140 g] diced yellow onion

½ cup [70 g] diced carrot

4 garlic cloves, minced

1 Tbsp fresh thyme leaves, minced

1½ tsp fresh rosemary leaves, minced

1 large egg

½ cup [120 ml] milk

¼ cup [65 g] ketchup

2 tsp Diamond Crystal kosher salt

1 tsp Worcestershire sauce

½ tsp soy sauce

2 Tbsp matzo meal

2 lb [910 g] ground beef, preferably 80/20
(80 percent lean beef and 20 percent fat)

1 recipe Melted Onions (recipe follows)

CLASSIC BROWN GRAVY

3 Tbsp unsalted butter

2 Tbsp minced shallot

3 garlic cloves, minced

½ tsp freshly ground black pepper

This is an homage to old-school diner meat loaf, rather than Mom's classic doused in ketchup. The homemade brown gravy makes it truly special and would be great over biscuits, mashed potatoes, turkey, or an old sock. The onions are a key element and add sweetness and acidity, so don't skimp. This comes together in less than an hour, so you can make it any night of the week. Serve with mashed potatoes, and save any leftovers for a meaty Raid-the-Fridge Reuben (page 27).

2 sprigs thyme

3 Tbsp all-purpose flour

1½ cups [360 ml] beef or chicken broth

¼ tsp apple cider vinegar

1 tsp soy sauce

½ tsp Diamond Crystal kosher salt

To make the meat loaf, preheat the oven to 350°F [180°C]. Cut off the crusts of the challah slices and use your hands to tear them into large pieces. Grind the pieces in a food processor to make fresh bread crumbs. Measure 2 cups [80 g] of bread crumbs and set aside. Store any leftover crumbs in an airtight container in the freezer for up to 2 months.

In a heavy-bottomed sauté pan, melt the schmaltz over medium heat. Add the onion, carrot, garlic, thyme, and rosemary and cook, stirring occasionally, until translucent and aromatic, about 5 minutes. Transfer to a shallow bowl and allow to cool. Set aside the pan for cooking the Melted Onions.

In a large mixing bowl, use a whisk to beat the egg, milk, ketchup, salt, Worcestershire, and soy sauce, until thoroughly blended. Add the fresh bread crumbs and matzo meal, and then stir the mixture with a wooden spoon or spatula until homogeneous. Add the cooled sautéed vegetable mixture and mix thoroughly to combine.

Add the ground beef to the mixture. Gently break up the meat with your hands, then mix all of the ingredients together just until they are distributed evenly. Don't overwork them, which will toughen the meat loaf.

Line a 9 by 13 in [23 by 33 cm] rimmed baking sheet with aluminum foil and coat the foil with nonstick cooking spray or a splash of vegetable oil. Transfer the meat mixture to the sheet, and form into a loaf shape about 7 by 12 in [17 by 30.5 cm]. Let the loaf rest while you prepare the onion topping.

Drape the onions evenly over the raw meat loaf. Bake the meat loaf for 55 minutes. It's done when it reaches an internal temperature of 160°F [71°C]. Make sure to let it rest for at least 10 minutes before serving. Meanwhile, make the gravy.

To make the gravy, in a large shallow sauté pan or cast-iron pan, melt the butter over medium-high heat until it begins to bubble. Add the shallot, garlic, black pepper, and thyme. Sauté until the shallot and garlic are softened and slightly browned around the edges, about 3 minutes. Whisk in the flour, and cook over low heat, stirring constantly, until the flour is well browned, about 3 minutes more.

Add the stock and whisk rapidly until the flour dissolves into the broth. Turn up the heat to high and cook, stirring often, until the gravy is thick enough to coat the back of a spoon, 3 to 4 minutes. Stir in the vinegar, soy sauce, and salt and remove from the heat. To serve, slice the meat loaf thickly and spoon gravy on top.

Melted Onions

2 Tbsp Schmaltz (page 56)

2 cups [280 g] thinly sliced yellow onion

2 sprigs thyme

1 sprig rosemary

1 Tbsp apple cider vinegar

1 Tbsp sugar

½ tsp Diamond Crystal kosher salt

In the sauté pan you used to cook the vegetables, melt the schmaltz over medium-high heat until it is bubbling. Add the onions, thyme, and rosemary, then cook until the onions just start to brown and have reduced in size by about 25 percent, tossing them occasionally so that they don't burn, about 15 minutes. You want to fry them to get good, even caramelization, but these aren't supersweet, slow-cooked onions. Raise the heat to high and add the vinegar, sugar, and salt. Sauté until the vinegar and sugar glaze on the onions nicely, 2 to 3 minutes. Remove the herbs. Makes about ¾ cup [150 g].

THE ALL-GROWN-UP YEARS

"Are You Pregnant Yet?"

No better excuse to eat . . .

. . . a Lot, Frequently, and Plenty of Pickles

"I'm wondering, but I'm not asking. I don't ask. Well, I did at first, but I don't anymore. I don't want to meddle! I'm not sitting around waiting for a phone call—but if the time ever comes, I'm going to love them to pieces."

—Evan's mom, on her future grandkids

Sometime around the dawn of your third decade, or within months of shacking up (whichever comes first), you start fielding The Question—from parents, grandparents, the guy at the corner store. "Soo, when are you going to start having kids?" It tends to happen around the same time you begin deliberating yourself: Do I have to have a kid? Will I be able to have a kid? Do I want to have a kid? I do! I don't. We do! We don't. I mean, we probably will? But can I wait until I'm fifty, like Janet Jackson? Or even forty-eight, like Rachel Weisz? (Hmm, not wise.) And if we do have kids, will our apartment be big enough? Will they be healthy? Will they be Jewish? Will we, as parents, turn into our parents? (Probably, yes.)

It's a big decision. One worth ruminating, over and over and over, as Jews are wont to do. And one, rabbis will tell you, the survival of the religion is riding on. Orthodox Jews, who make up roughly 10 percent of American Jews, have, on average, 4.1 kids per Jewish adult. At the other end of the Jewish spectrum is a growing segment: those born to Jewish parents who identify as having "no religion." They have only about 1.5 kids.

As Jonathan Sarna, professor of American Jewish history at Brandeis, explains, "The Orthodox have become the demographic 'engine' of the Jewish community. The non-Orthodox apparently forgot how to have children." According to Pew, the rest of us Jews aren't producing enough kids to replace ourselves. So, there's that. No pressure.

Women on the fence about growing a human inside your body, remember! There is an upside: For forty weeks, before your life is forever changed, you have a good excuse to down a Challah Grilled Cheese (page 213) and Babka Milkshake (page 210) every day.

Baby Naming

Jews love to name their children after beloved relatives, but unless you're Sephardic, those relatives must be dead. So no Isaac IIIs or Jacob Juniors. Same first letter, though, is fine. Bucking all the Jewish rules, my niece was bestowed with the middle name Frances while Grandma Frances was still very much alive. After a long pause, Grandma Frances decided she was flattered.

Tip: Don't tell your parents your future child's name until after the baby is out of your womb and in the world. "Hazel?" my mom said, making a face in the hospital room, until she looked at that face, and fell so hopelessly in love we could've named the baby Eva Braun and she wouldn't have blinked.

Old Jewish Names We Bet Will Never Come Back*

ADOLF
BARRY
DICK
Herschel

Beryl
HYMAN
IRWIN
MORT

Shlomo
GAY
MYRNA
STAN
MINDLE

*Wise Sons' delivery vans are named Harold and Ethel.
(It's a boy? See Bris, page 22.)

Wise Sons' Chocolate Babka

Makes 2 loaves

DOUGH

1 cup [240 ml] whole milk

1 package (2¼ tsp) active dry yeast

4¾ cups [665 g] all-purpose flour

1 cup plus 2 Tbsp [250 g] unsalted butter, at room temperature

1 Tbsp sugar

3 large eggs plus 1 egg yolk, at room temperature

1½ tsp vanilla extract

1 tsp Diamond Crystal kosher salt

FILLING

1 cup [200 g] sugar

3¾ Tbsp [19 g] unsweetened cocoa powder

2 tsp ground cinnamon

¼ tsp Diamond Crystal kosher salt

1½ cups [330 g] unsalted butter, at room temperature, cut into chunks

3 Tbsp water

1¼ lb [570 g] bittersweet chocolate, chopped to pea size, or use chips (we use 72 percent chocolate)

STREUSEL

¾ cup [105 g] all-purpose flour

2½ Tbsp granulated sugar

2½ Tbsp golden or dark brown sugar

½ tsp ground cinnamon

¼ tsp Diamond Crystal kosher salt

½ cup [110 g] cold unsalted butter, cut into 1 in [2.5 cm] cubes

Pastrami may have been the reason we started Wise Sons in 2011, but our babka instantly became a signature. This was long before Bon Appétit *magazine compared babka to a young Taylor Swift, "a niche figure ready for the crossover to mainstream star." Leo and I argued for days over what "authentic" babka was, both having our own ideas from childhood, as deli customers do. Eventually, we agreed on this refined version, swirled with 72 percent bittersweet chocolate covered with a thick layer of brown sugar streusel.*

To make the dough, warm the milk for 30 seconds in a small microwave-safe bowl. The milk should be warm, but not hot. Transfer to a medium bowl, and whisk in the yeast. Whisk in 1 cup [140 g] of the flour and let the mixture sit for 20 minutes, uncovered.

In the bowl of a stand mixer fitted with the paddle attachment, combine the butter and the sugar. Beat on medium speed for about 4 minutes, until well blended and pale yellow. With the mixer running on medium speed, add the eggs and egg yolk, one at a time, waiting until the first egg is fully incorporated before adding the next, and scraping down the sides and bottom of the bowl occasionally. Add the vanilla, and then the remaining 3¾ cups [525 g] flour. Add the yeast mixture and mix on low speed for 1 minute.

Add the salt and continue to mix until the dough starts to look ropy and the color is uniform throughout, about 2 minutes. When you pull the dough with your hands, there should be wide strands of dough that come away cleanly from the bowl. Remove the bowl from the mixer, cover with plastic wrap, and refrigerate overnight.

continued

To make the filling, whisk the sugar, cocoa, cinnamon, and salt together in a medium heat-proof bowl. Combine the butter and water in a medium saucepan over low heat and cook until the butter has melted and is beginning to foam. Pour the melted butter over the dry ingredients and mix well. Let cool until thickened.

Remove the dough from the refrigerator and divide it into two equal pieces. On a well-floured work surface, roll out one piece of dough into a 12 by 20 in [30.5 by 50 cm] rectangle. Cover edge to edge with half of the chocolate filling, and sprinkle on half of the chopped chocolate in an even layer.

Starting from the long edge farther away from you, roll the dough toward you tightly like a jelly roll. Fold the entire rolled log in half (it should be about 10 in [25 cm] long), and then twist a few times to make figure eights. This will create more swirls and reduce bready pockets. Repeat with the second piece of dough and the remaining filling.

Place each log in a well-buttered 9 by 5 in [23 by 12 cm] baking pan and let rest for 1 hour, until the dough rises just over the edge of the pan. Preheat the oven to 325°F [165°C]. While the dough is proofing, make the streusel.

To make the streusel, combine the flour, white and brown sugars, cinnamon, and salt in a medium bowl. Add the butter and mix with your hands until well blended and crumbly, with butter pieces the size of peas. Refrigerate until ready to use.

Cover the proofed babkas with streusel. (We like to cover them completely.) Gently press the streusel into the dough if you are having trouble getting it to stick.

Bake the babkas for about 1½ hours. The babkas will be a nice light brown color and pull away slightly from the edges of the pans when done. When tapped with your knuckle on the bottom, the cake should sound solid.

Babka Milkshake

Makes 1 milkshake

For the ultimate decadent frozen treat, start with a **thick slice of chocolate (or, gasp, cinnamon) babka**, cut into chunks. Combine them in your trusty blender with about **½ cup [120 ml] of milk** and a **squirt of chocolate syrup** (the classic Fox's U-Bet can't be beat), and pulse into a smooth purée. Add a heaping **scoop of vanilla ice cream**, straight from the freezer—you want it as cold as possible! Pulse until the mixture is smooth, but resist the urge to blend it more than necessary, because the resultant heat will melt your milkshake. (Nobody likes a liquidy milkshake.) Pour the thick, frothy mixture into a glass, frosted in the freezer if you're fancy. Garnish with **chunks of babka** and a **drizzle of syrup**.

Loaded French Toast

Serves 2 to 4

Superlative French toast is easy. Cut about four **1 in [2.5 cm] thick slices of challah** (page 125) and put into a large casserole dish. In a large bowl, mix up **6 eggs** with **¼ cup [60 ml] milk** and **¼ cup [60 ml] buttermilk**. The buttermilk is the ace up your sleeve here. Add a **splash of vanilla** (don't skimp on the real stuff), a **pinch of kosher salt**, and a **dash of cinnamon** and whisk it all up with a fork—because whisks are a pain to clean. Pour over the challah and use your hands to swish the challah around the mixture and ensure it is fully covered. Let the challah hang out for 10 minutes, flipping halfway for max coverage. The fatty bread is going to hold up nicely. You'll see!

Get a skillet hot over medium heat and add a big dollop of **butter**. Watch it start to bubble, swirl it, then carefully add a couple of slices of the soaking challah. Cook until golden on the bottom, maybe 5 minutes, and then flip and fry until cooked through. Repeat with the remaining slices.

Splurge on the **real maple syrup**, and don't be bashful with more butter and some **sliced fruit** if you have it. Try the peaches on page 46.

Challah Grilled Cheese

Makes 1 sandwich

Two ½ in [12 mm] thick slices challah, homemade (page 125) or store bought

1½ Tbsp Pastrami Jam (recipe follows)

2 slices American cheese

⅓ cup [40 g] grated aged Gruyère cheese

2 tsp mayonnaise

Heat a seasoned cast-iron skillet (a nonstick pan will do in a pinch) over medium heat for 5 to 6 minutes, until hot. Lay out the bread on a cutting board or a plate. Spread the jam on one side of a slice of challah, and top with a slice of the American cheese. Add the grated Gruyère, and the second slice of the American cheese. Spread the outside of the second slice of challah with half the mayonnaise, shmearing it from edge to edge. Place on top of the American cheese, with the mayonnaise side facing up, to close the sandwich.

Lower the heat to medium-low. Carefully pick up the built sandwich and flip it, placing the mayonnaise-slathered slice face down in the center of the skillet. Cook the sandwich, undisturbed, for 4 to 6 minutes, until the cheese begins to melt. (Lower the heat if needed.) While the first side cooks, carefully spread the remaining mayonnaise on the top slice of bread. Carefully flip the sandwich, using a spatula. Cook for 4 to 5 minutes more, using the back of the spatula to lightly press down on the sandwich to encourage browning and melting.

Remove the grilled cheese from the pan and transfer to a cutting board. Cut into triangles and serve hot.

Grilled cheese is the ultimate comfort food, but challah grilled cheese is heavenly. In our opinion, no other bread will do. We like the high-low combination of American cheese and Gruyère. The American cheese provides a perfect melty texture, and the Gruyère adds flavor and funk. Cooking grilled cheese with mayonnaise might sound goyish, but believe me: It yields the most perfect golden brown crust. And it isn't greasy or easily burned, like butter.

Pastrami Jam

1 Tbsp vegetable oil

2 medium yellow onions, diced

8 oz [225 g] pastrami, chopped (Don't trim the fat!)

½ cup [100 g] packed golden brown sugar

½ cup [120 ml] apple cider vinegar

¼ cup [80 ml] maple syrup

Heat a heavy-bottomed skillet over medium-high heat. Add the vegetable oil and heat until nearly smoking. Add the onions and cook for 5 to 6 minutes, until translucent, stirring often. Add the pastrami, stir, and cook for 3 to 4 minutes. Add the sugar, vinegar, and maple syrup and stir to combine. Bring to a simmer and cook until the liquid begins to thicken, 6 to 8 minutes, stirring as needed. Turn the heat to medium-low and cook for 1 hour more, stirring every 15 minutes to prevent sticking and burning.

Remove from the heat. Using a food processor or an immersion blender, process the mixture to a jammy consistency. Transfer to an airtight container and let it cool. Store, covered, in the refrigerator for up to 1 week, or in the freezer for up to 3 months. Makes 2 cups [600g].

Pickles for the People

Every deli-goer wants free pickles. Here's an idea: Why not make your own?

Sweet Brine

Makes about 2¼ cups [540 ml]

¾ cup [150 g] sugar

1 Tbsp Diamond Crystal kosher salt

1 cup [240 ml] apple cider vinegar

½ cup [120 ml] water

This versatile brine is very sweet, tart, and balanced.

Heat the sugar, salt, vinegar, and water in a small, heavy-bottomed saucepan over medium heat until the liquid begins to bubble, whisking once or twice to make sure the sugar and salt are dissolved. Cook for 30 seconds more and remove from the heat.

Pickled Beets

Makes enough to fill a 1 qt [960 ml] jar

1 large red beet (about 1 lb [455 g])

1 recipe Sweet Brine (left)

1 dried bay leaf

One 1 in [2.5 cm] cinnamon stick

4 whole cloves

4 whole allspice berries

⅛ tsp black peppercorns

Small pinch of chili flakes or whole dried chile de arbol

Pickles are the perfect foil in a sandwich with rich or smoky meat, or in a salad with creamy goat or blue cheese.

Preheat the oven to 400°F [200°C]. Tightly wrap the beet in heavy-duty aluminum foil and place on a rimmed baking sheet. Roast in the oven for 50 to 60 minutes, until cooked through. To check the beet for doneness, pierce with a small knife or skewer; it should slide in easily. Remove the pan from the oven, carefully open the foil, and let the beet cool slightly. When cool enough to handle, use a folded paper towel to gently rub off the skin and any blemishes. Transfer the beet to a cutting board and cut into 1½ in [4 cm] cubes or ½ in [12 mm] thick slices.

While the brine mixture is heating, put the beets in a clean 1 qt [960 ml] glass jar and add the bay leaf, cinnamon stick, cloves, allspice berries, peppercorns, and chili flakes. Slowly pour the hot brine into the jar and let the entire mixture cool on the counter until it reaches room temperature. Seal with a tight-fitting lid and refrigerate. The pickled beets will be ready to eat within 24 hours. They will keep in the refrigerator for up to 3 months.

Pickled Mustard Seeds

Makes a generous 2 cups [330 ml]

¾ cup [135 g] whole yellow mustard seeds

1 Tbsp mustard powder

1½ tsp smoked paprika
(also known as pimentón)

1 recipe Sweet Brine (page 214)

Serve these with Smoked Fish Salad (page 180), over latkes (page 33), or as an acidic, smoky condiment in any sandwich.

Add the mustard seeds, mustard powder, and paprika directly to the hot brine in the pan and simmer over medium-low heat for about 15 minutes.

Pour the mixture into a jar with a tight-fitting lid and let cool on the counter until it reaches room temperature. Seal and refrigerate. The pickled seeds will be ready to eat within 24 hours, but will get better with age. They will keep in the refrigerator for up to 3 months.

Pickled Red Onions

Makes enough to fill a 1 qt [960 ml] jar

1 recipe Sweet Brine (page 214)

1 lb [455 g] red onions,
   cut into ¼ in [6 mm] rings

1 whole star anise

One 2 in [5 cm] cinnamon stick

2 dried bay leaves

2 whole cloves

We serve these with our Chopped Liver (page 165), but they're great in sandwiches and burgers, or on their own.

While the brine mixture is heating, put the onions in a clean 1 qt [960 ml] glass jar and add the anise, cinnamon stick, bay leaves, and cloves. Slowly pour the hot brine into the jar and let the mixture cool on the counter until it reaches room temperature. Seal with a tight-fitting lid and refrigerate. The pickles will be ready to eat within 24 hours, but will get better with age. They will keep in the refrigerator for up to 3 months.

Pickled Cucumbers Bread & Butter Style

Makes enough to fill a 1 qt [960 ml] jar

1 recipe Sweet Brine (page 214)

12 oz [340 g] Persian cucumbers,
thinly sliced

1 cup [125 g] thinly sliced yellow onion

1 tsp brown or yellow mustard seeds

½ tsp ground turmeric

4 garlic cloves, peeled and smashed
with the flat side of a knife

These pickles are ideal with Egg Salad (page 181) or in a Big Macher Burger (page 74).

While the brine mixture is heating, toss the cucumbers and onions together in a small bowl to evenly combine, then transfer to a clean 1 qt [960 ml] glass jar and add the mustard seeds, turmeric, and garlic. Slowly pour the hot brine into the jar and let the entire mixture cool on the counter until it reaches room temperature. Seal with a tight-fitting lid and refrigerate. The pickles will be ready to eat within 24 hours, but will get better with age. They will keep in the refrigerator for up to 3 months.

Basic Brine

Makes about 1¼ cups [300 ml]

2 Tbsp packed golden brown sugar

2 Tbsp Diamond Crystal kosher salt

1 cup [240 ml] white wine vinegar

1 cup [240 ml] water

A classic.

Heat the sugar, salt, vinegar, and water in a small heavy-bottomed saucepan over medium heat until the liquid begins to bubble, whisking once to make sure the sugar and salt are dissolved. Cook for 30 seconds more, and remove from the heat.

Pickled Carrots

Makes enough to fill a 1 qt [960 ml] jar

1 recipe Basic Brine (recipe precedes)

1 lb [455 g] carrots, peeled and cut into ⅛ in [4 mm] coins

1 garlic clove, peeled and trimmed

1 Tbsp roughly chopped fresh dill

½ tsp black peppercorns

½ tsp yellow mustard seeds

A Wise Sons addition to our Cobb Salad (page 47), for crunch and acidic bite.

While the brine mixture is heating, put the carrots in a clean 1 qt [960 ml] glass jar and add the garlic, dill, peppercorns, and mustard seeds. Slowly pour the hot brine into the jar and let the entire mixture cool on the counter until it reaches room temperature. Seal with a tight-fitting lid and refrigerate. The pickled carrots will be ready to eat within 24 hours, but will get better with age. They will keep in the refrigerator for up to 3 months.

Pickled Green Tomatoes

Makes enough to fill a 1 qt [960 ml] jar

1 recipe Basic Brine (left)

12 oz [340 g] firm, green, unripe tomatoes, cut into wedges

5 garlic cloves, peeled and trimmed

2 to 3 whole allspice berries

2 to 3 sprigs dill

2 dried bay leaves

2 whole cloves

½ tsp black peppercorns

½ tsp yellow mustard seeds

The underappreciated, super garlicky, and tart "other" classic deli pickle.

While the brine mixture is heating, put the tomatoes in a clean 1 qt [960 ml] glass jar and add the garlic, allspice berries, dill, bay leaves, cloves, peppercorns, and mustard seeds. Slowly pour the hot brine into the jar and let the entire mixture cool on the counter until it reaches room temperature. Seal with a tight-fitting lid and refrigerate. The pickled tomatoes will be ready to eat within 24 hours, but will get better with age. They will keep in the refrigerator for up to 3 months.

The Kvetching Department

Where nostalgia reigns, prices are too high, and everyone wants free pickles.
An assortment of actual complaints from delis around the country.

- "I read the *NYT* and *WSJ* reviews on your website, but I didn't read the reviews in the California papers 'cause what do they know? Keep up the good stuff, but in the Mission?"

- "I should have known better when I saw half the staff is Asian."

- "It's time to turn in your Chinese Chicken Salad (CCS) vendor card. Your salad packaged in a plastic container was pathetic at best. You're like the Donald Trump of Chinese Chicken Salads. Turn in your CCS vendor license immediately."

- "Mazel on your Tokyo location. But matcha babka? Not authentic at all. Chocolate or cinnamon babka will sell just fine."

- "I am from the Bronx where my grandpa had a REAL neighborhood Jewish deli, so believe me, I know deli! The hubby is from Brooklyn so he knows deli, too. Well, this is def NOT Jewish deli!"

- "Seriously, kale salad at a Jewish deli? Oy. What's next, Kosher Kumbatcha (sic)? Please tell me that you're at least going to make up for this sacrilege by offering chopped liver. And don't forget the cheesecake."

- "When I lived in New York, getting good deli was about as hard as buying a newspaper. We now live outside Sacramento, where getting a good bagel is about as hard as getting a good newspaper!!"

- "For a community that loves pot stickers, gyoza, and pelmeni, there is no reason why kreplach would not sell if marketed effectively (in my humble opinion)."

- "I had matzo ball soup and a pastrami sandwich and all I could think was, 'This doesn't seem like a Jewish deli.' I mean, I've had more meat fall out of a NY deli sandwich than was in this one."

- "Matzo ball soup. It used to be stellar here. A rich, delicious broth with a giant, firm, and tasty matzo ball floating in the center. What I got yesterday was hot dog water."

- "Where's the warmth? The old Jewish man who talks to you and remembers your name?"

- "Stopped by to pick up some bagels on Sunday afternoon and they were freakin' out of bagels. How can a Jewish deli be out of bagels?"

- "For starters, you have to go through a TSA-style security check just to get in. Then, you get to pay $14 for *half* a pastrami sandwich."

- "Disappointing!! Overpriced! Publix sandwiches are much better!"

- "OMG! The manager is the spawn of THE SOUP NAZI from *Seinfeld*!!!!"

- "How dare the manager YELL at your customers and treat us like cattle. WE ARE NOT CATTLE."

- "I'm a lifelong New Yorker who recently moved to Florida. The potato salad was not edible. If that's homemade? Fuhgettabout it! Egg cream was nice."

- "Being a Jewish guy, I like Jewish food . . . There is NOTHING Jewish about this place. Or maybe one of the owners' mothers was twice removed or something."

- "The pickles were great. I just wish they would put buckets of them on the table for self-service."

- "I used to go here with my grandmother and her asinine son, also known as the family's toxic uncle. As a kid, the food was decent, but the service was terrible. I went back recently. The pickles were not fresh and the Bloody Mary tasted like stomach acid."

- "Warning: They DO NOT GIVE FREE PICKLES."

And occasionally, of course, customers kvell, too:

- "I have spent these past 20 years here looking for a good pastrami sandwich, and had pretty much given up hope—and then you guys came along! I will nominate you for a Nobel Prize in pastrami, should the Nobel Foundation add that category."

Shivah's Silver Lining

Free food delivered right to your living room

Jews Do Death Right

The best thing about the Jewish death ritual? Following a funeral, the first thing bereaved Jews do is eat. It's called the *seudat havra'ah*, the meal of condolence. Literal translation: "the meal of recuperation." Comfort food! A trend that can be traced back to the Old Testament!

Grieving Jews are showered not with flowers. "What good are flowers?" Great Aunt Esther once asked—but food. Lots of food. Enough to feed those in mourning, plus a living room full of friends and neighbors and frenemies for the next seven days. It's called "shivah." And somehow, long ago, our ancestors knew it was exactly what we needed when a loved one dies: A time to do nothing but mourn. To wail and cry and cry-laugh and maybe sneak a puff of cannabis in the bathroom. A time to be at home not futzing in your kitchen, as people pour in through the unlocked door, to serve and sweep and support and sit.

Death is devastating. Shivah isn't fun. And as Larry David, who wrote an entire Broadway play about shivah, once said: "It's incredible material." True. When my grandma Frances died in Florida, a few weeks shy of ninety-seven, the deli messed up the catering order and delivered, with all the pastrami and corned beef and knishes, its signature chocolate cake: THE KILLER, it read in red frosted script. We laughed, and then ate the whole thing, of course.

Every culture has its funeral food. Some have no qualms calling it such. For the Amish, it's Funeral Pie, a sweet cinnamon-raisin concoction. For the Mormons, it's Funeral Potatoes, a cheesy big-pan potato casserole, which, I've been told, supposedly kicks kugel's ass. There's the Irish Wake Cake. Mexicans have Bread of the Dead. Jamaicans cook goat curry by the gallon. Southerners make boatloads of fried chicken, and what Perre Coleman Magness, author of *The Southern Sympathy Cookbook* (2018), calls "that Pineapple Thing"—a cake made of canned pineapples, sugar, Cheddar cheese, and crackers.

For Jews, there's no special recipe. Supposedly, a shivah should include round items, like hard-boiled eggs, to symbolize the cyclical nature of life. But no one brings hard-boiled eggs. They bring homemade lasagnas in aluminum foil pans, catered cold cuts, Tupperware containers of hand-scooped cantaloupe, and a crazy amount of cookies. And mandel bread, more than anyone could ever eat in a lifetime, let alone in a week. Because if there is one item that says "shivah," it's mandel bread.

"There's no real food?"
—A Jewish father surveying the cookie spread at a recent shivah

Chocolate-Dipped Coconut Macaroons

Makes 12 cookies

4 egg whites, at room temperature

2½ cups [250 g] unsweetened shredded coconut

1½ cups [300 g] sugar

¼ cup [30 g] almond meal or flour

1 Tbsp honey

½ tsp vanilla extract

½ tsp Diamond Crystal kosher salt

4 oz [115 g] bittersweet chocolate, chopped

In a large nonstick saucepan, mix together the egg whites, shredded coconut, sugar, almond meal, honey, vanilla, and salt with a heatproof rubber spatula over medium heat. Cook for 5 to 6 minutes, stirring constantly and scraping the bottom and sides of the pan, until thick and sticky, and white streaks appear on the bottom. Transfer the mixture to a bowl to cool. (The dough will keep, tightly wrapped, in the refrigerator for up to 2 days.)

Preheat the oven to 350°F [180°C]. Line a baking sheet with parchment paper. Drop the dough onto the prepared baking sheet by the heaping tablespoon, forming tall, round domes that are evenly spaced. Bake for 18 to 20 minutes, until puffed and golden brown. Cool on the pan for 2 minutes, and then transfer to wire racks to cool completely.

Line a baking sheet with parchment paper. Melt the chocolate in a microwave-safe bowl in the microwave on full power: Start with 1 minute, stir with a spoon, and continue to microwave in 30-second increments until completely melted and smooth.

What to bring to a shivah? You could order a bunch of corned beef, or make a casserole; a chicken soup would be soothing. But the easiest, sweetest thing to do is bake.

Dip the bottom ¼ in [6 mm] of each cookie in the melted chocolate, setting the dipped cookies on the parchment-lined baking sheet. With the back of a spoon, drizzle the remaining chocolate over the tops of the cookies in a zigzag pattern. Refrigerate the cookies until the chocolate has hardened, about 10 minutes.

The cookies will keep in an airtight container at room temperature for up to 5 days.

Safta's "Mohn" Cookies

Makes 24 cookies

DOUGH

3 cups [420 g] all-purpose flour

¼ cup [35 g] poppy seeds

2 tsp baking powder

½ tsp Diamond Crystal kosher salt

1 cup [200 g] sugar

¾ cup [165 g] unsalted butter, at room temperature

2 large eggs

2 Tbsp fresh lemon juice

1 Tbsp grated lemon zest

1 tsp vanilla extract

TOPPING

⅓ cup [40 g] walnuts

¼ cup [50 g] sugar

½ tsp ground cinnamon

¼ tsp Diamond Crystal kosher salt

1 to 2 Tbsp room-temperature water

My safta baked a lot in her prime. Her mohn cookies—meaning poppy seed—were one of my dad's favorites when he was a kid. I love making them, and eating them, now.

To make the dough, whisk together the flour, poppy seeds, baking powder, and salt in a large bowl. In the bowl of a stand mixer fitted with a paddle attachment (or in a large bowl, using a handheld mixer), beat together the sugar and butter on medium-high speed until pale and fluffy, about 3 minutes. Scrape the sides and bottom of the bowl and the paddle with a rubber spatula.

With the mixer running on low speed, add the eggs, one at a time, waiting until the first egg is fully incorporated before adding the next. Add the lemon juice and zest and vanilla and mix until well combined. Scrape the sides and bottom of the bowl.

Continuing at the lowest speed, add the flour mixture and mix until a moist dough comes together. Scrape the bowl again to incorporate any remaining flour. Form the dough into two balls with your hands, and flatten them into disks. Wrap each disk tightly with plastic wrap, and refrigerate for 30 minutes. Meanwhile, make the topping.

To make the topping, grind the walnuts finely in a food processor. Combine with the sugar, cinnamon, and salt in a small bowl and set aside. Preheat the oven to 375°F [190°C]. Line two baking sheets with parchment paper.

Flour a work space and rolling pin. Remove one disk of dough from the refrigerator, unwrap it, and dust with flour. Roll out a rectangle or square until about ¼ in [4 mm] thick. Using a 3 in [7.5 cm] round cookie cutter, cut out the cookies and place them on the prepared baking sheets, about ½ in [12 mm] apart. Ball up any scraps of dough and repeat the process of rolling out and cutting the dough. Repeat with the second disk.

Brush each cookie with a little water and sprinkle generously with the ground walnut topping, about 1 tsp per cookie. Press the topping gently into each cookie with your palm.

Bake for 10 minutes, and then rotate the baking sheets and for bake 5 minutes more. The cookies should be firm to the touch and beginning to brown around the edges. Allow to cool completely on the baking sheets. The cookies will keep in an airtight container at room temperature for up to 5 days.

Mandel Bread

Makes 36 cookies

1⅓ cups [115 g] slivered almonds

3 cups [390 g] all-purpose flour

2 tsp baking powder

1 tsp Diamond Crystal kosher salt

1¼ cups [250 g] sugar

¾ cup [180 ml] vegetable oil

3 large eggs

1 Tbsp grated orange zest

1 Tbsp vanilla extract

1 tsp almond extract

The Jewish biscotti! Kind of. Mandel bread is often said to be bland. Ours is less bland, but it's still mandel bread! We take the traditional route—almondy and crisp, with a bit of grated orange. Best dipped in coffee.

Preheat the oven to 350°F [180°C]. Scatter the slivered almonds on a baking sheet and toast for 7 minutes until light brown. Remove from the oven and let cool on the baking sheet.

Combine the flour, baking powder, and salt in a large bowl and whisk to blend well.

In the bowl of a stand mixer fitted with the paddle attachment (or in a large bowl, using a handheld mixer), combine the sugar and vegetable oil, and mix until well blended, about 30 seconds. With the mixer running at the lowest speed, add the eggs, one at a time, making sure each one is fully incorporated before adding the next. Add the orange zest, vanilla, and almond extract and mix until well combined. With the mixer still running at the lowest speed, gradually add the dry ingredients and mix to combine. Scrape the paddle and the bowl with a rubber spatula to make sure there are no pockets of wet or dry ingredients, and continue mixing until you have a smooth dough. Add the toasted almonds and mix just until well distributed. Scrape the bowl one more time to bring all of the dough together into one mass. Cover the bowl with plastic wrap and refrigerate for at least 30 minutes, or up to 2 hours.

Return the oven to 350°F [180°C]. Line two baking sheets with parchment paper. Divide the dough roughly in half using a rubber spatula. With oiled hands, pick up half the dough, form it into a log, and transfer the dough to the center of one of the parchment-lined baking sheets, positioning the log parallel to the long sides of the pan, with at least a few inches of space between it and the edges of the pan. Continue to lengthen the dough into a log about 11 to 12 in [28 to 30.5 cm] long and 3 to 4 in [7.5 to 10 cm] in diameter. Repeat with the other half of the dough on the second baking sheet. Flatten the top of each log slightly, and if the dough has become tacky, oil your hands once again and smooth the logs.

Bake the logs until firm, about 25 minutes, rotating the baking sheets front to back and switching racks halfway through to ensure even baking. Transfer the logs to wire racks and let sit until cool enough to handle before proceeding. Leave the oven on so it is hot for the second bake.

Transfer one cooled cookie log onto a cutting board. Using a serrated knife, trim the ends of the baked log, and then slice into ½ in [12 mm] thick cookies. Place the cookies on one of the parchment-lined baking sheets, with a cut-side down. Repeat with the remaining cookie log. Bake the cookies for 10 minutes in the 350°F [180°C] oven. Flip them over so the other cut side is facing down. Bake for about 10 more minutes, until all the cookies are dry, crisp, and nicely browned. Transfer to a wire rack to cool.

The cookies will keep in an airtight container at room temperature for 1 week.

Rugelach

Makes 40 cookies

1 cup [220 g] European-style unsalted butter

½ cup plus 2 Tbsp [150 g] cream cheese

1½ cups [210 g] all-purpose flour

½ tsp Diamond Crystal kosher salt

½ cup [120 ml] room-temperature water

4 Tbsp [60 g] turbinado or coarse sanding sugar

You've got the option of three different fillings here: tart apricot, a salty-sweet walnut filling, and a rich chocolate one. If you want to make two flavors, halve the ingredients for each filling. These are the crumbly rugelach made with cream cheese dough, which are different than the yeasty Israeli variety.

Remove the butter and cream cheese from the refrigerator about 15 minutes before making the dough to soften. In a medium bowl, whisk together the flour and the salt. Set aside.

Cut the butter into large chunks and add to the bowl of a stand mixer fitted with the paddle attachment (or to a large bowl, if using a handheld mixer), and beat the butter on high speed for 1 minute until creamy. Scrape down the sides and bottom of the bowl with a rubber spatula, add the cream cheese, and continue beating until thoroughly combined. Scrape down the bowl again. With the mixer on medium-low speed, add the flour mixture and mix until a soft dough comes together into one big, rough piece.

Stretch out a large piece of plastic wrap on your counter. Gather the dough into one ball with your spatula and place in the center of the plastic wrap. Tightly wrap and then form into a rectangle roughly 6 by 5 in [15 by 12 cm]. Refrigerate until firm, at least 2 hours or up to 24 hours. (At this point, the dough can be placed in airtight container or resealable plastic bag and frozen for up to 2 months.)

Remove the dough from the refrigerator and cut into four equal pieces. Work with one piece at a time, keeping the remaining pieces in the refrigerator, wrapped in plastic, until ready to use. Flour the piece of dough well and flatten with your hands to warm up the edges slightly and prevent them from cracking. On a well-floured work surface, using a floured rolling pin, roll out the dough into a rectangle roughly 9 by 12 in [23 by 30.5 cm]. The dough should be thin and nearly translucent. Transfer the dough to a sheet of parchment paper, place on a baking sheet or large platter, and refrigerate. Repeat the process to roll out the remaining dough, laying each rectangle on a sheet of parchment paper and stacking the sheets on the baking sheet in the refrigerator.

Arrange the first rectangle of dough with its parchment paper on your work surface with a long side near you. Trim both long sides of the dough to achieve straight edges. Fill with walnut, chocolate, or apricot filling as in the following instructions.

Brush water on the border of the dough to help it seal. Roll up the dough very tightly into a log, moving from the long side closest to you to the side farthest away, and ending with the seam tucked underneath the log. Brush the log with some of the water, and sprinkle the entire log liberally with 1 Tbsp of the turbinado sugar. Transfer the log and the parchment paper onto another baking sheet and place the pan in the freezer. Repeat the process with the three remaining sheets of dough, stacking them on top of one another in the freezer.

Line a baking sheet with parchment paper. Remove the first log you rolled from the freezer and trim the ends to expose an evenly filled spiral. Slice the log with a sharp knife at 1 in [2.5 cm] intervals. Transfer the slices to the prepared baking sheet, spacing them about 1 in [2.5 cm] apart. Continue with the remaining logs in the freezer until all the cookies have been trimmed, sliced, and arranged on the baking sheet. Freeze the entire pan of cookies for 1 hour. (After the cookies have completely frozen, they can be stored in airtight container in the freezer for up to 2 months.)

Preheat the oven to 350°F [180°C]. Place the baking sheet with the still-frozen cookies in the oven and bake for 25 to 30 minutes, rotating halfway through for even browning. Transfer the cookies to a wire rack to cool. The cookies will keep in an airtight container at room temperature for up to 1 week.

Walnut Filling

Place **1¼ cups [150 g] of chopped walnuts** on a baking sheet and toast for about 12 minutes, until fragrant and glossy. Grind the walnuts in a food processor until they are as fine as granulated sugar. Mix the ground walnuts with **¼ cup [50 g] packed golden brown sugar**, **¾ tsp Diamond Crystal kosher salt**, and **½ tsp ground cinnamon**. You should have about 2 cups [200 g] of filling. (The filling will keep in an airtight container in the refrigerator for up to 1 week, or in the freezer for up to 1 year.) To make the **rugelach**, follow the previous instructions, but when you are ready to fill the dough, brush the surface of the rectangle with water. Spread out ½ cup [50 g] of the filling evenly over the dough, leaving about a ½ in [12 mm] border along the long side farthest away from you. Roll and sprinkle with **sugar**, as described previously. Repeat with the remaining dough and filling, and proceed with the recipe.

Apricot Filling

In a small saucepan, combine **1 cup [160 g] of chopped, dried apricots** and **¾ cup [180 ml] of water**. Bring to a boil over medium heat, cover, and turn down the heat to low. Simmer for about 5 minutes, stirring occasionally, until all of the water has been absorbed and the apricots are soft. Transfer to a food processor and add **¼ cup [60 ml] of water**. Blend until a smooth, thick paste is achieved. You should have 1 cup [240 ml] of filling. Refrigerate until ready to use. To make the **rugelach**, spread ¼ cup [60 ml] of the apricot filling evenly over one rectangle of dough with a rubber spatula, leaving about a ½ in [12 mm] border along the long side farthest away from you. Roll and sprinkle with **sugar** as described previously.

Chocolate Filling

To make the **rugelach**, follow the previous instructions, but when you are ready to fill the dough, brush the surface of the rectangle with **water**. Spread out **½ cup [90 g] of mini semi-sweet chocolate chips** evenly over the dough, leaving about a ½ in [12 mm] border along the long side farthest away from you. Roll and sprinkle with **sugar** as described previously. Repeat with the remaining dough, spreading out ½ cup [90 g] of chocolate chips each time, and proceed with the recipe.

THE SNOWBIRD YEARS

Return to the Sunshine States . . . .

Ruminations on retirement

Will We Head South, Though?

Like we said, the Jewish snowbird tradition has been going strong for almost a century. (See "Visiting the Grandparents in the Sunshine States," page 42.) At this point, our retirement community roots run deep. As descendants of, say, the Fountains or Boca Grande, the Polo Club or Palm Canyon Estates, we can't help but feel an allegiance, a seemingly inevitable generational pull to settle, as seniors, beneath palm trees. To kibitz poolside. To play bridge.

It makes sense, in a way. These gated, predominantly Jewish communities have become like the modern-day American equivalent of our ancestors' Eastern European villages. The gates themselves perhaps erected, not so much to keep others out, but rather to keep Jews in, as August Wilson might say. Together, in a world where we are otherwise spread thin.

And these communities keep proliferating, says Dr. Ira Sheskin, who studies the demography and geography of Jews at the University of Miami. "What happens is, the sixty-somethings who move in eventually turn seventy-five, eighty—and sixty-year-olds don't want to hang out with eighty-year-olds! And so they build new communities."

Some Jews can't wait to get to the Floridian gates. "God's Waiting Room," my cousin calls it. Others are choosing to retire in less expensive sunny places, like North Carolina or Nevada or Arkansas (Arkansas?).

And yet, what does the future hold for Jews of our generation? For those who prefer the wilderness to water aerobics, seasonally driven restaurants to "Italian Night" clubhouse buffets? We will still crave community, of course, but from side-by-side condos overlooking the third hole?

If we retire to Rome, we can drink Brunello and sit on park benches! If we retire to Silicon Valley, we can cycle along the coast and launch tech startups! If we retire to Alta, Utah, at age eighty, we can ski for free! (It used to be seventy, but too many people were taking advantage of it.) And if we retire to New York or LA or San Francisco, we can become docents at the museums and make 5:00 p.m. reservations at all the best restaurants and sink the last of our savings accounts into exorbitant rents!

Maybe, one day, armed with the ability to get everything from fresh bagels to hair dressers to vitamin D delivered to our door; and play online canasta from our couch; and take Gentle Hatha Yoga via VR; and summon driverless cars to whisk us to the movies, to the grandkids' graduations, to the lecture series featuring a gray-haired Lena Dunham—maybe then the allure of the gated golf community, as we know it, will have waned.

And, maybe, instead, we'll cluster with wizened friends, old and new, in sustainably built high-rises in a second-tier city or in tiny prefab homes in some beautiful field, and . . . walk and talk and lounge around the pool, plotting what to cook for dinner.

Dayenu

The Candle-Lighting Service, a.k.a. Acknowledgments

If you've been to Wise Sons, there's a good chance you've met my parents, Linda and Stuart, who camp out to kvell for hours to anyone who will listen. It annoys the hell out of me, but I know they're just being prideful Jewish parents. Thank you, Mom and Dad. This book, or business, would not have happened without the culture you instilled in me, the education you provided for, and the unwavering support you've always given.

My Safta and Saba would be disappointed that this book is not kosher, and my Nana would be terrified she appears in photos she wouldn't think are glamourous, but they'd be proud that we're connecting to our culture and sharing it with the world.

To my brother, Ari, who has been the recipient of a lot of my stress—thank you for always supporting me and helping make this business go!

Thank you to everyone at Chronicle Books for your enthusiasm for *Eat Something*, especially Tyrrell Mahoney and Sarah Billingsley. Thank you Deanne Katz for your thoughtful edits, attention to detail, and openness to our unconventional approach. Thank you Margo Winton Parodi for making sure the recipes read clearly. Thank you Vanessa Dina and Sara Schneider for cover and design work, to Steve Kim and Tera Killip for terrific production, and to managing editor Magnolia Molcan.

Thank you to Maren Caruso for your creativity and commitment to our vision. Thanks, too, to our amazing on-set team of Jillian Knox, Robyn Valarik, Jennifer Thomas, Josh Lewis, Kristene Loayza, and Daniel Hulbert. Thanks to Ali Cameron for everything. And thank you Carolyn Schneider for your help and hands, and for being the best mother-in-law on set.

And to Rachel and George, my partners in crime, who have poured themselves into this book and created something so personal. From the moment we set out on this journey, it has never felt like work. Thank you to Super Agent Danielle Svetcov, who guided an anxious duo of Jewish writers through their first cookbook.

Thank you to the Wise Sons Team, who amaze me every day. We are nothing without our employees. Joey, my Culinary Captain, who worked through many of the recipes with me and prepared food for the photo shoot. Zac, for your deep thinking and wordsmithing. To Cassidy, archivist extraordinaire and babka model second to none, and to Anna and Eric for offering their recipe expertise on recipes where I didn't have it.

And thank you to my wife, Jessica, who is a true BO$$ and never flinches when I come home tired and anxious about deadlines or have to whip up a few last-minute recipes. She's there for me through thick and thin, and there would be no *Eat Something* without her.

Rachel, here. Ditto to everyone and everything Evan said. Double thanks to Sarah Billingsley, a true Jew at heart, who got it, and us, from the start. Thank you to Danielle Svetcov for championing this book, and me, and for making both of us better. Thank you to Maren Caruso for that goddamn gorgeous brisket. Our weeklong photo shoot was as bonding as Jewish summer camp. And to George McCalman, my co-regular, my other husband, and a supreme talent who helped make *Eat Something* everything we hoped it would be.

Thank you to all the friends, family, and fellow Jews I called upon for input on everything from sick days to Chinese restaurants to dating, including Dave Rubenstein, Josh Sternlicht, Josh Sens, Cousin Dave, Jourdan Abel, Rachel Zarrow, Rebecca Flint Marx, Camille Mason, Dara Solomon, Jason Israel, Lauren Gersick, Raina Wallens, and Peter Orner. Thanks to Rabbi Ryan Lamberg and crew for two decades of San Francisco seders, to my cousin Emily for being such a yenta, and to Ryn Singley for being such an unlikely Jewophile. Thanks to Erica Weiss for her annual latke bar and to Wendy Spero for her hilarious take on the Christmas tree, and to all the tweenagers who took the time to type or talk about everything from bat mitzvahs to kids' tables. Thanks to everyone at Camp YJ, deep in the hills of New Hampshire, who shared care package tactics and more. And to my nephew, Jonah Richter, and his parents, for throwing such a blowout bar mitzvah at just the right time.

Thank you to Uncle Matthew and Manhattan Sammy's for giving me a college summer job and some deli-counter cred. Thank you to my grandparents, whose tables and voices were especially vivid while writing this book: Grandma "How many bawls do you want?" Frances; Grandpa "What do you want for breakfast? Bagels, cream cheese, and lox?" Sam; Grandma "Would like a to-mah-toe?" Hannah; and Grandpa Orrin, who sent us home with fresh bread every Sunday. (And to think I begged for Wonder Bread.) I miss you and your mini-Rachel loaves. Thank you to my husband, Josh, for everything, including your first and always close reads. And to Hazel and Oren, my two favorite people to feed.

Thank you to Annabel and Syl, to Doctor Mike Herzlinger for his flawless iced coffee, and to my sister, Julie, for allowing the photo on page 65 to be published. Thank you to my mother for her meatloaf and so much more, to my father for teaching me the Art of the Over-Order, and to them both for unintentionally supplying so much material for this book. I love you.

And, lastly, thank you to Evan, for bringing me into this meaningful project in the first place. It was fun, wasn't it?

Image Credits

Images on the Title Page and pages 31 (top), 36 (Left), 66 (top left – Evan), 68 (top left), 68 (top right), 104–5, 156–57, 159, 188 (Second from top), 188–89 (top middle), 189 (top right), 228 (middle left), 228 (bottom left), 228 (bottom right), 229 (top left), 231 courtesy of the Bloom family.

Image on page 189 (bottom right) of Barry and Nancy Freeman (Toronto, ON), 1960, courtesy of Ontario Jewish Archives, Blankenstein Family Heritage Centre, Accession 2018-7-8.

Image on page 203 of Baycrest Women's Auxiliary membership tea (Hamilton, ON), Oct. 1967, photograph by Bochsler Studios Ltd., courtesy of Ontario Jewish Archives, Blankenstein Family Heritage Centre, fonds 14, series 4–9, file 8.

Image on page 188 (Second from bottom) courtesy of the Bendett family.

Images on pages 22–23, 25, 39 (top), 39 (middle left), 39 (bottom left), 78–79, 86–87, 128, 132–33, 146–47, 207, 229 (bottom left) courtesy of the Boujo family.

Image on page 73 of Camp Shalom (Gravenhurst, ON), 1991, courtesy of Jewish Archives, Blankenstein Family Heritage Centre, Accession 2007-12-2.

Image on page 174 of Chabad Pesach fair (Toronto, ON), 1986, photograph by Graphic Artists, courtesy of Ontario Jewish Archives, Blankenstein Family Heritage Centre, item 4427.

Images on pages 228–29 (middle) and 229 (top right) courtesy of the Leo Baeck Institute, New York.

Images on pages 60–61, 63 , 66 (middle left), 66–67 (middle bottom), 68 (second from top right), 68 (middle left), 71 courtesy of Daniel Moneta.

Images on pages 184–85 and 188 (middle left) courtesy of Diana Rothery Photography.

Images on pages 42–43 and 52 courtesy of Emily Berman.

Image on page 64 courtesy of Erica Weiss.

Image on page 149 of Frankel family Rosh Hashana dinner, 120 Isabella St. (Toronto, ON), ca. 1900, photograph by Herb Nott & Co., courtesy of Ontario Jewish Archives, Blankenstein Family Heritage Centre, fonds 104, file 5, item 5.

Images on pages 68 (second from bottom right), 228 (top right), 229 (middle left - Diet Coke), 229 (middle right) courtesy of the Galant family.

Images on pages 28–29, 39, 66 courtesy of the Gelfand family.

Images on pages 96–97, 135, 175 courtesy of Hillel at Stanford, Stanford University.

Image on page 45 (bottom left) courtesy of Jeff Gersick.

Image on page 72 courtesy of Jenna Grauman & Joseph "Chicken" Goodman, Camp Alonim.

Images on pages 45 (middle) and 228 (middle right) courtesy of Joanne Abelson.

Images on pages 188 (bottom right) and 189 (second from top right) courtesy of the Katz family.

Image on pages 116–17 of Krugel family Shabbat dinner, ca. 1940, courtesy of Ontario Jewish Archives, Blankenstein Family Heritage Centre, accession 2018-4-4.

Image on page 189 (bottom left) of Ladovsky family wedding dinner, Kielce, Poland, 1930s, courtesy of Ontario Jewish Archives, Blankenstein Family Heritage Centre Fonds 83, file 9, item 12.

Image on page 188 (bottom left) courtesy of Mara Sohn.

Image on page 179 of Max Hartstone (center) with Crown Bread Company customers and staff (Toronto, ON), ca. 1952, courtesy of Ontario Jewish Archives, Blankenstein Family Heritage Centre, accession 2017-10-5.

Image on page 220 of men at cemetery in Eastern Europe, ca. 1900, courtesy of Ontario Jewish Archives, item 3755.

Image on page 99 of Mimi Wise cooking cabbage rolls (Toronto, ON), 1959, courtesy of Ontario Jewish Archives, Blankenstein Family Heritage Centre, Fonds 16, item 7.

Image on page 119 of Morris family Shabbat (Toronto, ON), ca. 1930s, courtesy of Ontario Jewish Archives, Blankenstein Family Heritage Centre, item 3262.

Image on page 38 (bottom) of Purim play, Temple Tikvah, St. Catharines, Ontario, ca. 1970s, courtesy of Ontario Jewish Archives, Blankenstein Family Heritage Centre, accession 2009-5-4.

Images on pages 31 (middle), 39 (bottom right), 45 (top left), 45 (top right), 45 (middle left – pool kids), 45 (middle right), 65, 66 (bottom left), 68 (bottom middle), 68 (bottom right), 188 (top left), 189 (Second from bottom right), 204–5, 206 courtesy of Rachel Levin.

Image on page 189 (top left) of Sam Ross, Rabbi Shoime Langner, and Rabbi Moishe Langner at Simcha, Torath Emeth Synagogue, Viewmount Ave., Toronto, 1958, courtesy of Ontario Jewish Archives, photo #4500.

Image on pages 176–77 of Shopsy's Delicatessen 40th anniversary, Spadina Avenue, 14 August 1961, courtesy of Ontario Jewish Archives, Blankenstein Family Heritage Centre, item 4996.

Image on pages 188–89 (middle) courtesy of the Simmons family.

Images on pages 107, 189 (middle), 228 (top left) courtesy of Stanford University, Ira Nowinski Collection.

Image on page 173 courtesy of Sussman family.

Image on page 38 (top left) courtesy of Valerie Bishop.

Images on pages 45 (bottom right) and 229 (Bottom Right) courtesy of Wendy Spero.

Index